RUNNING FOR BETTER

A story about running to live and think better

Preface: Book Content

My story isn't anything special. I'm not an elite athlete. I don't have tales of victories or feats of ultra-endurance to share. I have no glorious redemption from the depths of drug and alcohol abuse to describe. Like most people, I've hovered somewhere in the middle, with some successes and failures but mostly just above or below average. From my early twenties, the passing of each season had marked a slow slide away from reaching my potential. Then, over the course of a year, everything changed.

It all started with boxing training. It gave me the push I needed to start climbing the steep hill to fulfil my potential. It snapped me out of a lull and made me dig deeper than I ever had before. Since then, it has been running which has taken me furthest. At the age of thirty-four, it made me ask myself many tough questions while whispering answers at the same time. Over three years, five marathons and many miles later, I've learned to listen better.

I've charted my progress through simple stories and lessons learned from mistakes and successes in playing sport, boxing and later running. Each one is underpinned by a practical philosophy to help benefit the training and mindset of any endurance athlete. Training for marathons has developed my endurance but also given me the strength of mind to better other areas of my life. Once we know how to get the best out of ourselves in one area, there's no reason why we can't apply those techniques to other parts of our lives.

I don't know where you are on that hill to reaching your potential, but if you are reading this I'm assuming you want to learn to become a better athlete. This book offers you a way to apply your running for a better life.

Brian Kearney, October 29th, 2017

Preface: Book Format

Your time is valuable, so I have broken this book into short stories that are lessons, or reminders, of how endurance training can help us to live and think better. Each story is intended to improve elements that are vital to endurance athletes such as routine, motivation and mindset. They cover the time training for my first two marathons in Cork and Dublin. It's the book I would have wanted to read when I first started running and the book to which I will return whenever I need a reminder of what it takes to run and live better.

This book is best read in order, but the Table of Contents is organised like a reference section so that you can find the parts that might be of more interest to you.

Table of Contents
Running for Better: Book I

Part I: Why Do You Run?..8
Chapter 1: Journey Ending and Beginning 9
Motivation: Why do I run?.. 9
Focus: Know where you want to go and keep going 12
Part II: My History 17
Chapter 2: Back to the Start..18
Mindset: The ingredients of endurance 18
Self-Discipline: The power of hard work 19
Courage: Practice pressure... 19
Self-Awareness: What works today might not work tomorrow 21
Self-Awareness: Know what you need... 22
Consistency: Be prepared for all conditions 23
Courage: Endure to prevail... 24
Chapter 3: Going Around in Circles 27
Routine: Living easy hits hard eventually 27
Mindset: Learn how to train your mind 28
Mindset: Keep your shape 28
Mindset: Big egos lead to big falls... 30
Motivation: All decisions have consequences 31
Attitude: There's no growth in comfort... 34
Routine: Fresh mornings lead to full days 36
Part III: Getting Back Up - Boxing to Running 38
Chapter 4: A Round in Boxing 39
Direction: The right coach knows when to push and pull.......................... 39
Progress: Take it slow and steady until you are ready 39
Recovery: Sometimes the cure is the cause... 43
Mindset: Relax to allow room to improve 47
Direction: Review your progress... 49
Mindset: Knowing our weaknesses can make us stronger.......................... 50
Progress: Sow what you want to grow 50
Direction: When you're lost, slow down and find a guide 51
Routine: Run early and make the day taste better 52
Progress: Sometimes the best way forward is the simplest 53
Chapter 5: A Running Start..55
Race Report: Charleville Half-Marathon 55
Attitude: Enjoy the process 59
Race Report: University of Limerick Half-Marathon 60
Chapter 6: Connecting the Dots..65
Routine: Always find time and space to move 65
Race Report: Clontarf Half-Marathon.. 66
Challenges: Take them one at time 72
Mindset: Be open to inspiration 74
Chapter 7: Finding a Better Way 76

Routine: The perfect plan is the one that works for you...........................76
Mindset: Tomorrow is always a fresh start 77
Routine: Take the time to learn how to do things right 78
Routine: Prioritise and value your time 79
Part IV: Getting Better – Living well 81
Chapter 8: Living Plan..82
Living Well: Find the filter for your essentials 82
Living Well: Add value by taking away...84
Chapter 9: Living the Way..86
Focus: Focus on what you can control...86
Mindset: Find a blueprint for success 87
Mindset: Remember what is in your control 89
Alcohol: Don't let today take from tomorrow..90
Routine: Have a morning routine 91
Motivation: Be ready for excuses...93
Chapter 10: Training for Speed 95
Consistency: Focus on the process not the goal 95
Performance: Practice under pressure...96
Recovery: Stay in tune with mind, body and circumstances 98
Recovery: Do your best to do things right 99
Direction: The less we want to examine our actions, the more likely it is that we need to do it..101
Chapter 11: Running the Way 103
Self-Awareness: Know, and work, on your strengths and weaknesses......103
Nutrition: Learn from your mistakes...107
Part V: Running and Learning 109
Chapter 12: Running Free 110
Recovery: Never let go easily...110
Race Report: Cork City Marathon...113
Running Tip: Running Form 116
Running Tip: Secret technique 117
Attitude: Celebrate effort, not the passing of time....................................122
Consistency: The Next Step...125
Lessons from Cork marathon 126
Running for better - Book II: Cork to Dublin City Marathon 129
Chapter 13 - Back to Thailand..130
Consistency: Expect that life will not always go to plan............................130
Chapter 14: Back To Boxing..132
Mindset: Stay steady until you get stronger...132
Chapter 15: Finding Air 136
Attitude: Look for solutions, not excuses 136
Chapter 16: Finding Answers in Vietnam..139
Gratitude: Remember that being free enough to run is to be rich 139
Recovery: Your body is a puzzle for you to figure out..............................140
Chapter 17: Competition Time..143
Performance: Competition should bring out the best in us......................143
Race Report: Charleville Half-Marathon 144

Running Tip: Run in blocks 146
Challenges: Consider what it takes to commit 148
Mindset: Don't compare yourself to others, be inspired by them 150
Attitude: Face whatever you fear... 151
Running Tip: Hold the Hills 152
Routine: Dig deep to find space for bigger blocks 152
Chapter 18: Countdown to DCM 154
Routine: A good routine only needs small changes 154
Recovery: Keep your head and do your best 155
Chapter 19: Marathon Review 157
Challenges: Anything worthwhile takes some pain to achieve................. 157
Race Report: Dublin Marathon 158
Courage: Are you ready? 160
Epilogue 162
Author's Note 163
Appendix: Overcoming Challenges... 164
Lessons from Dublin Marathon 165
How can we overcome challenges and learn from them? 166
Stoic Resilience: Anticipate 166
Stoic Resilience: Accept.. 168
Stoic Resilience: Adapt 170
Stoic Resilience: Act.. 172
Stoic Resilience: Adjust 176
Bibliography/ Reading List... 180
Acknowledgements 182

PART I: WHY DO YOU RUN?

CHAPTER 1:
JOURNEY ENDING
AND BEGINNING

Motivation: Why do I run?
Chai Lai Elephant Camp, Northern Thailand, 2013

Dusk falls over our simple cabin in a lush green forest where we can hear the low murmur of grazing elephants. Spiralling sounds of cicadas puncture the air after a heavy rain shower. It's an environment far removed from home, but some things remain the same: a fresh T-shirt, faded shorts and a pair of socks are bundled on a chair in a corner of the cabin. My muddy runners are a source of odours that can only be matched by the jungle so have been exiled to the steps outside. I'll fumble for them bleary-eyed at dawn before running through the hills of the Northern Thai 'Golden Triangle' region, once famous for its production of poppies for heroin.

When I wake up, it's so early that there is barely any light around the camp. The air is cool, but it won't be for long. My senses, sweat and heart-rate will rise with the steep hills that will greet me along the way. It will be tough, but the run needs to be run; the miles don't wait for anyone.

I put on the fresh socks, T-shirt, well-worn shorts and well-travelled runners: that's all I need to feel better. Happiness doesn't have to be complicated. I tie my runners with a double knot in case they unravel. That was one of the first rules of running that I learned through experience: take your time to always double-knot.

The routine of running is familiar but everything else is so different: the people, the weather, even the smell of the air. I'm the strange one here: a sunburnt 'Paddy' plodding along the side of isolated country roads. Instead of wide-eyed Irish cattle gazing back from the fields, there are elephants carrying tourists in the morning and logs in the afternoon. When the locals notice me, I witness the full gamut of human facial expressions: some seem stern to the point of anger, others totally ignore me but most delight in the sight of this strange man running around for no apparent reason.

One of the first foreigners to volunteer and live in the area had described to me the consternation she had caused when she first started her morning jogs. Concerned locals assumed she needed help or was fleeing some form of crisis. "Why are you running?" they asked. It was a perfectly valid query, but no matter how she much she tried to explain, they were never convinced by her answers. When she asked me the same question, my response didn't come as easily as I would have expected. I eventually reply "Enjoyment. I enjoy it". It's a simple answer that harbours so many untruths.

So much of running is not enjoyable: lungs that burn in the middle of a speed session, reddened ears whipped by a cold wind that cares not a jot for my plight, legs that ache with many miles to go and chafing in areas so intimate that I had forgotten their existence. Motivational posters never feature quotes on washing wet, sweaty gear or fumbling in morning darkness for that second sock while your partner blissfully sleeps in your warm bed. Running has made me question my sanity on early mornings, doubt myself on start-lines and vomit at finish-lines, but I keep looking for a better answer to that question: Why do I run?

A week later and it's time to fly back to Ireland. An afternoon flight from Bangkok brings us, my girlfriend Angie and me, back to the world of timetables, to-do lists and jobs. After two months of travel, we are leaving behind carefree lives to ones with schedules and responsibilities. I turn my attention to the tiny screen in front of me. It informs me that there are four thousand miles still to travel on our flight. My tired mind flicks it way through the latest Hollywood offerings until I stop at what appears to be a straightforward documentary on swimming. It turns out to be something very different: an incredible story of endurance that tracks the efforts of a well-known journalist, Diane Nyad, to swim the 110 miles (180 km) of hazardous, dark waters from Cuba to Florida without a shark-cage. Four failed attempts over the course of thirty-five years and still she keeps going. Her determination and persistence are inspiring and humbling but with each failure, I offer her silent excuses to end her struggle. Her fourth attempt has to be cut short as she drools in delirium from numerous paralysing man-o'-war jellyfish stings. I wince in my padded seat while sipping my gin and tonic, surprised by the emotion lodged in my throat. It's like watching a punch-drunk boxer still swinging for the title. After each attempt, she seems broken but comes back for more. Most of all, I ask 'why?' Why does a successful woman in her sixties still push herself to such extremes?

The documentary eventually unfolds a story of childhood abuse which scarred her deeply but forged a resilience that I couldn't begin to comprehend. It's not her athletic prowess, but her capacity to endure which inspires me most. It's unlikely that I'm ever to going to face the threats of sharks, lethal jellyfish or hypothermia, but what are the limits of my endurance? Is the ability to endure the recipe for resilience and a better life?

I'm hemmed in at the window seat with Angie dozing beside me. My thoughts and elbows need somewhere to go. Reverie and a second gin and tonic make me look inward for answers and I take out a pen. Right now, all I have is questions. How can I reach my potential as a runner and a person? Why do I run? I try to answer what seem like the easier ones first.

Why do I run? I enjoy it. What do I enjoy? It's those few seconds when my breathing feels easy, my body is strong, and my mind is clear. Then it's gone again and it's only when it's gone that I become aware of it. It's fleeting but fulfilling. It's enough to keep me going without chasing for more. I know it will come back.

How can I reach my potential as a runner and a person? I have written this book to better answer that question for me and for you.

Focus: Know where you want to go and keep going

My regrets in life are few but I often think of the progress I could have made if I had chosen running before my early thirties. Maybe you've always been a runner or an endurance athlete, but I had rarely strayed from team sports. Even when I did start running, if my steps had been traced, you would have seen busy patches of footprints all criss-crossing each other but would then stop dead in the middle of nowhere. The tracks would appear again a few months later, further back, but ending in the very same way. When I wasn't playing team sports, running was something I did to take me somewhere else, to make me fitter, to reach a goal. Once I achieved what I had set out to do, I would stop and not run again for months. It was like pushing a rock halfway up a hill and then letting it roll back down. My haphazard preparation for my first half-marathon will give you an idea of my attitude to running at that time.

A season of soccer had just finished and there were almost two months to spare before I went travelling for the summer, so I decided to train for the Cork City Half-Marathon. After a few weeks of running three times a week with steady improvement, I believed I was in shape to run a decent time. However, I wasn't so dedicated that I would let a few weeks of training get in the way of a good party. When a group of friends arranged a weekend away just before the race – which was on a Bank Holiday Monday – I didn't think twice about going. We rented a house near Dingle in County Kerry which is a little part of the world that seems to have its very own climate and time-zone: a change in the weather is never too far away and nights always seems to go on that much later. By the time I returned to Cork on the Sunday afternoon I was feeling very delicate and took my tired body straight to bed neglecting to pick up my race number.

When I peeled myself out of bed the next morning, I had to dash over to the City Hall and plead with the organisers to provide me with a number to race. They were unimpressed by my unusual request as they had closed entries the day before. They eventually dug up my number, but my morning got worse from then on. Missing the last shuttle bus taking runners to the start-line in Mahon left me four miles from where I should have been. With only forty minutes until the race started, I took off on what would have been a lengthy warm-up jog. I was beginning to have doubts about even getting to the start, not to mention running over thirteen miles. Knowing my legs weren't up to running seventeen miles (twenty-seven km), I stuck out my thumb in a desperate attempt to share the workload. Almost immediately some 'Good Samaritans', avid runners, picked me up and dropped me near the starting line, greatly entertained by my bumbling preparation.

Another short jog from where I had been dropped off and I made it with a few minutes to spare. I looked like I had just finished the race: panting, sweating and red-faced with my hands on my knees. I spotted a good friend, 'Dinger', who I had known for years from school and playing on the same football teams. Dinger wasn't sweating: he was cool and calm, sipping on a sports drink and going through some light stretches. He took pity on me and gave me the last of his sports drink. I shook my head and braced myself for the tough miles ahead. *At least I'll sweat out the alcohol*, I thought. *It's too far to turn back anyway.* In the end, I had enough stamina to carry me through but there was no elation afterwards; I was too tired and dehydrated to wish for anything but a shower and my bed.

On the slow walk home, I wondered how much faster I could have run if I had committed more to the race. My time was relatively decent, under one hour thirty minutes, but I knew I hadn't trained or raced to my potential. How much better could I run if I committed to it? Could I have kept up with Dinger if I hadn't gone to Kerry? He had similar natural ability to me but once the starting gun went, it was the last I saw of him. *Could I catch him another day if I kept up the training?* I was at a point in the middle of the hill towards reaching my potential, but those questions faded away as I set off backpacking for nearly three months. Travel, at that time, meant a few beers every day and plenty of late nights so, after weeks of training, I let my fitness roll like a boulder back down to the bottom of the hill.

My attitude or discipline never seemed to point me in the right direction long enough to harness my potential. Just when it was time to push on to the next level, I would always go off and do something else. I was living a full life, but I wasn't living to my fullest. Diane Nyad's body had given up many times, but her mind never did. She was toughened from fourteen-hour training swims and her resolve held steady even through the wildest of storms.

If I was to live my best life, I needed to train my body and mind to start reaching towards my potential. The rest of this book is about how I found a way towards leading a better life, that anyone can follow.

The book is best read in order but if you are a busy runner and just want to start with my commitment to running, skip ahead to chapter 5. You can come to the earlier chapters later if you wish. 'A Running Start' covers my training and races, before getting into how I developed my mental strength. The intervening chapters chart my future development as a runner through team sports and boxing. Every section of every chapter provides a takeaway lesson that has benefitted my physical and mental training for sub-3-hour marathons.

PART II: MY HISTORY

CHAPTER 2: BACK TO THE START

Mindset: The ingredients of endurance

As athletes, we build our bodies to physically endure the demands we make on them, but how often do we think of training our minds in the same way? We strengthen our legs with a long run every week, but how do we know if our minds will last when we push them further than ever before? When we are at the bottom of a hill or stuck halfway up, what do we need to work our way to the top?

Starting out on any hill, we can't begin without courage and then consistency to keep going. Later, it takes self-discipline to push on or hold back and self-awareness to find a pace that suits us. We need to get the mix right and keep reinforcing it through training. It wasn't until I started running that I realised how important those ingredients of endurance were, but if I had looked a little deeper, I would have seen that they had been there all along.

The following stories are like little snapshots from my past that were left undeveloped in a locked drawer. Once brought to light, they formed a jumbled collage that ended up with running but started somewhere different in team sports and boxing. The details aren't as important as their purpose: reminders and lessons in how to run, live and think better. See them as a guide to reach your potential and to avoid making my mistakes.

Self-Discipline: The power of hard work

The sports in which I competed as a teenager were the Irish games of hurling and Gaelic football (GAA). To play with your GAA club is more than just putting on a jersey; it's about representing your town, your tribe, your family. My father and uncles had all played and talked about little else when together. They were the sports I was born into. I started with my club at the age of seven as did almost all of my friends. As we grew older, they were the games that we played every weekend and talked about every Monday.

Hurling is a game with everything that a sport should inspire in and require of its players: agility, courage, speed of body and mind and, above all, skill. Even the basic skill of hitting the baseball-sized sliotar is an art. Unfortunately, I wasn't an artist. Other players could pluck the ball from the sky and lash it sixty metres in the other direction in one fluid motion, while my technique was awkward. To be competitive, I had to make up for my lack of skill with an abundance of effort. I chased and harried. I cleaned up the dirty ball lying loose on the ground. More than anything, I ran a lot. As I became fitter, I was picked in positions – wing-back or midfield – where I could use my stamina and dogged persistence to support the better players around me. In contrast, when it came to schoolwork, I had more natural ability, so I tried to get away with doing as little as possible. Having to work hard at hurling taught me how to make up for what I didn't have.

Courage: Practice pressure

When I was fourteen, I graduated to a team one grade above my age group which was coached by my father. His methods and training style could be described as an 'old-school' approach. Training was more about developing character than technique. If players weren't willing to hit or be hit, they were never chosen to play. He would not tolerate lack of effort; we had to play with 'fire in our bellies'. His belief was that talent without passion would melt under pressure.

<u>Journal Entry: Dad</u>

Even though Dad was busy with a full-time job and five children under fourteen years of age, while my mother worked part-time, he still found time to coach different underage teams. I owe him my determination to give my all when it counts the most. Through him I have learned how much passion can power us forward if we control it in the right way. He has also shown me that you can combine a ferocious desire to compete with the ability to be calm and thoughtful. In a house filled with his books and notebooks, he was the first influence on my early reading and writing habits. I will be forever shaped by his early examples of passion, the desire to learn and the determination to do your best.

My dad's general demeanour was usually very calm but that changed in the dressing-room before an important game. His pre-match speeches could make the four walls around us shake a little. Tables, hurleys and gear-bags all bore the brunt of his passion at some point. We were never left in any doubt that we were expected to play with courage and determination, and to persist through pain.

If match day was a furnace, our mettle was forged in games at the end of training. They were a way for him to see how ready and able we were to perform under pressure. They came after practice drills which were never intricate or sophisticated but merely served as a calm before the storm at the end. We practised under pressure of different match-day situations: a goal down with a minute left, a point down with seconds left, a last-minute penalty: pressure and response. There was no let up as ball after ball rained down on the small square in front of the goal. If we couldn't perform well in training, we wouldn't survive on match day. Train hard, hit hard and get back up. We had to experience pressure to know if we could withstand it.

Self-Awareness: What works today might not work tomorrow

My style of play at that time was very narrow in its range, but it was effective – until one day it wasn't. What worked up to a certain level was brutally exposed at the next stage. The harshest lesson I have ever learnt as a player happened at the highest stage of competition I had experienced at the time. I was fifteen years of age and that sweltering day is still burned into my memory over twenty years later. It felt like I was playing in a furnace. My headgear was suffocating as I couldn't find space to breathe. Sweat trickled down my forehead and stung my eyes. But the player I was marking wasn't sweating. Every time he got the ball, he was getting by me like a cool breeze. I was only beginning to catch my breath when I realised how good this guy was. I didn't have enough experience to steady myself and the job of marking him was eventually given to someone else. By that stage the damage was done, and we lost the game. Fitness and determination weren't enough to compensate for my limited skills when they were stretched to the next level. It was a severe lesson that exposed all my weaknesses and told me that I needed to become a more balanced player, both mentally and physically. Luckily, the right people came along to show me the way forward and taught me lessons that would last me a lifetime.

Self-Awareness: Know what you need

A year later, still rough around the edges, I was called up to start training with the age group above me. We had a new coach and manager who brought a sense of purpose to everything we did. Our coach, 'Northern Joe', simplified the complicated. He repeatedly instructed and drilled us on the basics of the game, wanting us to get the basics right, make them instinctive and then play from the heart. The same elements were repeated and reinforced in different ways during every training session. He reminded us all the time that we had to have a balance of elements to be a true hurler in his eyes. He called them the four HS: head, heart, hurling, hunger and stamina. We needed heart to play with courage and hunger to keep coming back for more, to strive to get better. We needed the skills of hurling to outplay our opponents and stamina to keep doing it. At all times, we had to think about what we were doing and keep our heads, no matter what happened during a game. He still wanted 'fire in the belly' but also wanted 'ice in the mind'.

Northern Joe placed importance on how we behaved as well as how we played. He took a different approach to any other coaches we'd had up to that point. His language was clean, and his training gear was always equally immaculate. Clean play, no retaliation to dirty play and no bad language were all part of the instructions he delivered before every match. Although his voice was soft with a Northern Irish lilt, he always spoke with a passion that was wrapped around a steely determination. He made it clear that we were never to take a backward step, never to let anyone 'get at you'. If ever we were fouled against, he told us, "Keep your head, play fair and wait for your chance; when it comes, take man, ball and all." Take hits, keep your head but hit back twice as hard. For someone like me who didn't have a foundation of natural ability to rely on, here was a blueprint on how to perform at my best and every match and training session was another chance to get better.

Consistency: Be prepared for all conditions

"Train as you play, boys," we were told over and over. Before, during and after our training drills, he would demonstrate what he wanted or didn't want from us. Whenever we did training drills, he required us to do more than hit the ball. He wanted us to think about how and where we were hitting it, the pace we were putting on it and even the sound it made. "I want to hear it snap, boys!" He wanted us to imagine that each time we caught or hit the ball, we were in a match situation, surrounded by opposing players. "Attack that ball. No holding back!"

Northern Joe never wasted any words, but it took me a long time to fully understand some of them. Because his voice was soft, whenever he had to give us instructions from across the pitch, he had to cup his hand around his mouth to make himself understood. It was even harder to hear him when it rained; on those occasions he would stand in the middle of the pitch with his peaked cap drawn down tight over his eyes. As the wind drove the rain sweeping across the pitch, with the sound of dozens of sliotars snapping and whizzing back and forth for training drills, we would hear his voice calling out, "Pray for more rain, boys!" When a frigid wind was driving heavy drops of rain into my eyes and down my neck while I tried to catch a sodden ball dropping from grey skies, all I could think was: *feck him and his rain*. I hadn't yet understood that he wanted us to taste a little misery, to get stronger from it and to be ready for it on match day.

We never felt nervous before matches because we had already trained so hard and knew what we had to do. We just had to put all the pieces together and hurl with heart and hunger while keeping our heads: preparation and clarity. As a teenage boy, I always wanted to take the shortest, easiest route possible, but he was asking us to take the longest and toughest way around. We all groaned about it at some point, but the same messages were being repeated and embedded: train as you play, no surprises, pray for rain. The tougher and rougher the training, the harder to beat we became.

Courage: Endure to prevail

We remained undefeated for two years and had arrived at the highest possible stage: the premier grade final in the city and county of Cork. The last team we had to face were far bigger, older and stronger and were strong favourites to win. We were a country club up against a big city team, Na Piarsaigh. No one had expected us to be able to compete at this grade. Even members of our own club had voted against us stepping up to this higher grade after winning promotion the previous year. Our status as underdogs galvanised us even further and created a 'siege mentality'. We had trained as hard we could, but this match would require us to dig even deeper.

Just before the start of every game our manager, 'Big Con', would say a few words of motivation on the field. Con and Joe were a great combination, but they were very different men. While Joe never wasted a word, the breadth of Con's speech matched the considerable expanse of his waistline. His anecdotes were liberally shared and were nearly always punctuated by the lifting and adjusting of his trousers. As an orator, he could draw from a depth of knowledge in history, politics, poetry and hurling. No matter what the setting, a punchline and a chuckle were never too far away. His lofty quotes often went over our heads but as we huddled together, arm in arm, in the driving rain before this final match, he delivered a line that I have remembered ever since. He was standing in the middle of the group, wearing a fisherman's hat, a trench coat and a pair of wellingtons. His voice boomed from deep down as he told us that whatever happened that day we would walk away victorious. All we had to do was remember that 'It is not those who can inflict the most but those that can suffer the most who will prevail.' He paused for a moment, looked us all in the eye and added that these were the words of a Corkman, Terence MacSwiney, who died while protesting on hunger strike in an English prison. Plucking such a line from Irish history stunned us but the sentiment was very clear: victory to those who can endure.

By the time we formed a single line behind the marching pipe band we were ready to take whatever might be thrown at us. Our age and size should have counted against us, but it just made us try harder. We recklessly threw ourselves into every tackle, which seemed to unnerve our bigger opponents. We conceded some soft goals but kept coming back. The match ended in a draw and it took a second day to try to separate us on the scoreboard. Every time we were down, we kept coming back. The replay ebbed and flowed but we always seemed to be chasing the lead. In the end, we ran out of time.

After the final whistle, I sank to my knees and threw off my helmet. I would have cried but I just felt numb. We had given everything until there was nothing left. Some supporters dragged me to my feet. We were told to stand up and stand tall; they were proud of us. Back together in the dressing room, we all had our heads down. Con and Joe wouldn't accept tears or regrets and told us to walk away with our heads held high. They had seen us grow from boys to young men over the course of two years. They shook each of our hands in turn. We didn't have a cup in front of us, but the real prize was what we had learned and practised in our time together. Con and Joe had laid out the stepping stones to guide us and even though I have lost track of them many times, they have always been there waiting to point me in the right direction.

CHAPTER 3: GOING AROUND IN CIRCLES

Routine: Living easy hits hard eventually

When I turned eighteen, life began to take me elsewhere and away from the structure of training with my club. It started with university in a different county to study languages and then abroad to work and study in France and Spain. A few years of wandering took me teaching in South Korea and travelling throughout Asia and Central America. I stayed active in South Korea playing football and soccer – even winning the Asia Gaelic Games competition twice with Seoul Gaels – but I was training and playing less, socialising more and still expecting to be at my best. Everyone else was doing the same so I hardly noticed the slow slide away from my potential.

When I got back to Ireland, training with my local football and hurling club again quickly told me how far I had regressed. The morning after my first training session, I couldn't believe the pain in my legs from doing lunges, and that was just from the warm-up. Whenever we ran speed drills, instead of praying for rain I was praying for them to end. I was twenty-five years of age and should have been in my prime, but over the course of seven years I had let my performance drift further away from my potential than ever before. I had long lost sight of a path I had once been on; it was time to try to find it again.

Mindset: Learn how to train your mind

After some hard winter training on heavy pitches, I began to regain strength in my legs. As the soft ground hardened coming into spring, I noticed a sharpness that I hadn't felt in a while. I was fit and keen to get back playing competitive football. For our first championship game of the year I played well, and a local newspaper picked me out as the 'man of the match'. There were days when everything came easy when there was a flow to my play. However, my form could vary from game to game. I knew that my ability as a player didn't change from week to week, so it had to be my mental game that was letting me down. Awareness of how influential my mind could be, was the trigger to start training it.

Ice in the mind, fire in the belly. What came naturally as a teenager, I needed to find again: playing by instinct but thinking clearly. It was important to get the balance right, otherwise it resulted in either over-eagerness or over-thinking on the field of play. I tried visualisation techniques to map out what I wanted to replicate in a game, imagining myself catching cleanly, kicking clearly and moving smoothly. It was a worthwhile experiment, but when it came to match day, it felt as if I was crowding my mind instead of clearing it. Some days I was playing with the right amount of fire, other days not enough or too much, but with every game I was trying to better prepare my mind.

Mindset: Keep your shape

My first season back petered out before it really had a chance to begin: knocked out in the middle of the summer. A new season was a chance for a fresh start with change in team management, but my enthusiasm was soon blunted when I was dropped immediately from the team. The manager was trying out more conservative players in my position. I responded by playing the way I always had, attacking from the back, but with even more drive and determination. I tried to play in a way that would be impossible to ignore; taking chances, defending by attacking and kicking scores but it just made things worse and kept me on the side-lines.

After a few months with no progress, I became disillusioned and would often end up going for drinks before practice matches and training sessions. Hungover yet defiant, I sometimes played even better. I was in the moment, playing by instinct, but I was driven by anger and gradually losing my shape as I let my emotions get the better of me. A sharing of views with the manager helped clear the air but left me none the wiser on how to improve. Second-guessing my instincts to play how I thought he would have wanted, I became more defensive and cagey; a shadow of a player holding his position but adding nothing to the team. The greater good is always the team, even when it doesn't suit your individual strengths, but not being at my best wasn't really helping anyone.

Even when I picked up an injury, I was thinking only of what the manager would say or think. "Out injured again?" Managers accept your word with a nod and a slap on the back, but you fade from the picture. An injured player ceases to be who they are: someone who plays. Instead, I kept training, not mentally strong enough to say that my body needed a chance to heal. Playing on led to worse injuries: my efforts to steer clear of the 'no man's land' on the injury table just kept me there for longer.

Mindset: Big egos lead to big falls

Another unsuccessful season passed with more frustration than enjoyment, but I decided to stay positive for the year ahead. Training hard, I kept my head down instead and played in whatever position I was picked. In team sports, it can be a huge advantage to be adaptable enough to play in various positions and I was often selected to provide cover between back, midfield or forward positions. I wanted to nail down my preferred position as a wing-back but had to fill in wherever I was needed. In contrast to the previous season, I didn't let myself get frustrated. Wherever I was selected, I tried to play as well as I could.

There seemed to be a turning point after a league match when the management team apologised for taking me off when I'd been playing well at midfield. They said that the team performance had suffered afterwards, stated how much they valued me and told me how important a player I was for the team. Relief. My doubts were wiped out and my ego sated. I could relax now and just play my own game. However, five days later it was all over.

Management had picked me in another new position, changing me from midfield to corner-back. The player I was marking didn't appreciate me beating him to the ball and had thrown a several punches and elbows into my face without any caution from the referee. Eventually I hit back, a melee ensued, and I was the one booked for retaliation. The manager switched me to another position, but my focus was gone at this point: blinded by the frustration at not playing my best and angry that I had stooped so low as to be trading punches instead of kicking scores. The final ignominy was being called ashore soon after by the manager.

Throwing fists, getting booked, being taken off: this wasn't the player I used to be. Three seasons of training and yet I was playing and feeling worse than ever. All these thoughts swirled around my mind like a dark cloud, as I walked to the side-line, staring blankly, hands clasped on my head. The water I threw on my face did little to wash away the mix of dried blood, dirt and sweat. My eyes betrayed the emotion that lay beneath. Putting too much credence in praise and promises, my ego had set me up for a painful fall.

After that game, I had lost all belief in myself and management. Filling gaps in the team had only created cracks in my confidence and resilience. Training and playing football and hurling had once got the best out of me, but I felt I was stuck, not getting any better. It was easy to blame other people, but I had left my ego and factors outside of my control, affect me. It was a costly lesson, as that was the last time I ever played with my club, but one that eventually made me a better runner.

Motivation: All decisions have consequences

Backpacking in Asia for three months put my disappointment in perspective and returning in September felt like a fresh start. Despite having a long, lazy summer, I wanted to get back playing sports. Gaelic football was my real passion, but soccer was a chance to be involved with a team again. It was the obvious option as playing and training in a team environment was the only structure I knew. It was straightforward to fall into regular training and matches. The next few years followed the same pattern of summers travelling and winters playing soccer.

Travelling was the main highlight of each year and ranged from backpacking around Asia to volunteering in Colombia. I tried to stay active for at least some part of each trip – hiking, kite-surfing or cycling – but the travelling lifestyle blunted the edges of the fitness that I had built up over the winter. One summer I took off on a road trip with a good friend, Munson, who was living in Barcelona. We started out hiking for a few days in the Los Picos de Europa mountain range in Cantabria, which we always finished by supping cool beers and devouring three-course meals before enjoying whisky and cigars. We promised ourselves that we would hike or run early and then do some upper-body training in the afternoon, but that enthusiasm soon faded as we looped into the Basque country. After three weeks of travel, we fully embraced the late-night culture in Basque cities like Bilbao and San Sebastián and the only running was from the bulls in Pamplona.

When Munson had to return to Barcelona, I felt I needed a fresh challenge and decided to cycle part of the Camino de Santiago along the Northern Way which hugged the northern coast of Spain. Munson dropped me off at a sports store on his return to Barcelona and I bought the cheapest mountain bike, bike rack and pannier bags in stock. After getting everything ready later in the hostel, I tentatively set out the next morning along the Asturian coast. My lack of forethought became almost immediately obvious. I had chosen a mountain bike to handle off-road cycling, but the route was almost entirely on smooth secondary roads with very few dirt tracks. My sturdy mountain bike had thick tyres that dragged on the hot asphalt. The high price I paid for a cheap bike was a chain that would slip intermittently and jar my leg while I pedalled. It was manageable at the beginning, but after three days of cycling it was incredibly painful. My backside was also suffering in the saddle; no matter how much I changed position, I had to stop and stretch every hour or so. The pain called for desperate and inventive uses of a towel which didn't help much; neither did cursing my chain as it slipped going up some of the steeper hills I met on my way.

As my legs built up strength crossing from the northern region of Cantabria into Asturias, things became a little easier. The purchase of a gel saddle instead of my makeshift padding also helped; I didn't think a backside could be grateful but mine was very thankful. After nine days of cycling, I made it to the end of the pilgrimage route in the capital city of Galicia, Santiago de Compostela. The city and cathedral were beautiful, but it didn't seem right to stop when there was still road left to travel: another fifty miles (eighty km) and I would make it to where Galicia meets the Atlantic Ocean at the 'end of the world', Finisterre.

Early the next morning, I stole out of the slumbering city and kept pedalling until I couldn't go any further. Looking out on water that didn't stop until the Americas was a fitting end to the trip, along with ample servings of *pulpo a la Gallega* (octopus) and a bottle of Albariño white wine. I had tasted the best of the north of Spain over several weeks and was satisfied that I had regained some fitness before my return home.

My first jog back in Cork told me how sadly mistaken I was. Any notions that I had maintained my fitness were cruelly dismissed. Long lunches, late nights and slow miles on a pampered saddle were of little use to my legs on the hard road. Whenever I returned to running, it was like a map telling me how far I had drifted off course. The way back it was showing me was too hard, too long to follow; I was still looking for short-cuts.

Attitude: There's no growth in comfort

Instead of going where running wanted to take me, I went back to playing soccer. Playing with a team was the easier option: everyone else was just as unfit starting off the season, so I was never pushed out of my comfort zone as we built up our fitness. We had matches most Sundays and usually trained once or twice a week. It was enjoyable, but I was only regaining the ground I lost every summer.

If we had no match on a Sunday, I would still meet my old friend Dinger to keep him company in the middle of some ridiculously long runs. My endurance was poor, so I would last only a few miles and go back to bed to recover from the run, and the night before. He always encouraged me to keep at it, but it was easier to pretend that I didn't need that kind of endurance as a soccer player. Running just seemed too much like hard work.

Playing soccer was comfortable because I never had to push myself too much. I could enjoy a few beers every day during the summer, go out for drinks a few times every week during the winter and still have a place on the team. I didn't have to make any sacrifices and contentedly drifted from game to game without ever asking myself if I could be playing better. It took some running and a dry summer in Morocco to push me in the right direction.

Journal Entry: Waking up with running
Essaouira, Morocco
June 2012

Really enjoying Essaouira so far even though there isn't much to do at night. There aren't many bars, so I've kept to the odd few beers for sunset. In the morning, my head feels clear and I don't hide from the early light. Morning is the quietest time in the medina as the town only begins to waken and heat up only after ten o' clock. From my hotel room, I can smell the sea-air and pastries that will be a part of my day: the beach and breakfast. But first, I start my new morning routine, running.

It felt great this morning, jogging through the narrow, dusty lanes in between the high walls of the medina. Traders were setting up their stalls, but it was too early for them to catch me for a sale. I picked up the pace near the market centre which brought me out past the pier and then along the promenade by the windswept beaches. I'll be back on that beach later trying to kite-surf. Yesterday, I spent most of the two hours falling off the board or being pulled sky-ward by the kite like a rag doll. It was frustrating, but I need to keep practicing the little steps to get better.

This morning, I saw some of our instructors out kitesurfing for fun, way out at sea in the wilder morning winds. They were twisting and spinning over waves before launching themselves into the air. Watching them held me spellbound for a few moments. They were pushing their boundaries, balancing on the edge of brilliance. I shuddered when I thought of my own efforts the previous day, so clunky and laboured with only a bellyful of seawater to show for my efforts. Running seems easy in comparison. It gave me a burst of inspiration for the last couple of miles. It felt good to run along with a heavy bass-line that I could hold on to, Rock the Casbah *by The Clash (2manyDJs remix). It pulled me along with a smile for the last kilometre. This running lark isn't so bad.*

Routine: Fresh mornings lead to full days

Running in Morocco was a catalyst for greater clarity of mind and purpose. Morning runs with a clear head were a fresh start that I wanted to maintain. Back home, I made a more consistent effort at soccer and cut back on the late nights. Even though I started soccer training twice a week with some running, I still wanted to do more. When a friend suggested joining him for a conditioning class in a boxing gym, I signed up and loved it from the first night.

The physical part of the training was very tough: skipping, shadow boxing, punching drills, pad-work and conditioning exercises all packed into an hour. At the beginning, there were sessions when I couldn't tell my left hand from my right and if I could, I would have struggled to lift them. No matter how tired we were, we still had to try to replicate punching combinations while working with partners on boxing pads. It was easy to look foolish when you didn't get them right, so we had to concentrate even when we were exhausted. Unlike slow laps on a mucky field, boxing doesn't have space for hiding in the pack or cutting corners.

After around six weeks of conditioning classes, my progress carried over to the soccer pitch. Not only did I have a higher level of fitness but also a different mindset. I wasn't afraid of straying from my central, holding position because I knew I had enough energy to recover. Instead of conserving my energy to last the full ninety minutes, I was playing at higher intensity from an earlier stage of the game. Even when I was out of breath, I was still strong enough to make the right decisions. I remembered what it was like to play with a sense of flow, without holding back.

The contrast in intensity between boxing and soccer training became more pronounced with each week. Boxing was a tough hour that pushed body and mind the whole way. In contrast, soccer training dragged on for much longer, but we did far less. The players were all sound lads, but the muck and dirt of our dark pitch didn't entice many of them out on winter nights. Getting fitter made me realise how much I had fallen back, and I didn't want to let myself slide again. Boxing was going to push me further again but first it was going to knock me down.

PART III: GETTING BACK UP – BOXING TO RUNNING

CHAPTER 4: A ROUND IN BOXING

Direction: The right coach knows when to push and pull

After every boxing session, it felt like we had nothing more to give. Our arms, back and torso were either under tension or powering punches for so long that it was very easy to get sloppy and loose with our technique at the end. The better coaches knew when to push but also when to pull back. One coach, Tony, was particularly astute and I hung on his every word. He reinforced the same ideas in every training drill: breathing, form, stance, focus. The importance of smooth, dynamic movement was underlined – being hard to hit was just as important as hitting hard. He simplified boxing down to the 'boxing line' – getting out of your opponent's line of attack and into the best position to attack or defend. Even though the combinations could be confusing, he reminded us that they were just ways of attacking and defending ourselves. It had been a long time since I'd had a coach that spoke with such simplicity and clarity. I had missed that influence without even knowing but it was about to send me down a path that I couldn't have imagined.

Progress: Take it slow and steady until you are ready

"Everybody has a plan until they get punched in the mouth" (Mike Tyson)

Tony was always trying to improve our fitness in the conditioning classes but also to develop our boxing skills. By springtime, much of the training group had progressed to some very light sparring sequences - punching at half-strength or just with leading jabs. Getting into the ring to spar was the next step. The first evening that I fought in the ring, I couldn't believe how tired I felt after five sloppy one-minute rounds. By the last round, I could barely raise my hands to defend myself. Punching too hard too soon left me tired and unable to defend myself later. I had believed myself to be in good condition but being 'fighting fit' required a far higher level of fitness and better use of energy. After a few sessions, I learned to pace myself to keep punching up till the last round; getting hit in the head tends to make you learn fast.

As I became more confident, I felt more fluid and my leading left arm naturally dropped into a low guard. I wasn't doing it intentionally, but it was a technique which I didn't have the experience to use properly. It was like sprinting before I could jog, and it was about to cost me dearly.

At the end of another hard session, I was chosen to spar with a taller fighter inside the main ring. Tony was refereeing and told us to stick to jabs for the first minute. My rangy opponent peppered me with punches from a safe distance. Any time I tried to break the boxing line, it earned me a few warning shots that sent me backwards. Tony must have felt some sympathy as he told us we could box whatever way we wished for the next minute. It was a sloppy smash of leather, spit and sweat but the adrenaline kept us coming back for more. Tony called out, "Thirty seconds left, lads. Box all out!" I was breathing heavily but wanted to keep going until the end. I could hear that little voice of my ego again, *you're boxing well; just keep punching, put him under pressure. The coach is impressed. You've got this.*

    I paced forward, throwing out more punches, feeling loose, looking for the space to land a big one. Time ticked down. 9 ... 8 ... 7 ... I felt stronger as I drove him into the ropes. He was crouching down. 6 ... 5 ... 4 ... He closed his eyes and turned back on his right side. Then I saw it, but it was too late; a big arching punch looping up from low down. It crashed into my jaw sending me to the canvas. 3 ... 2 ... 1. The sparring session was over. I got back up straight away, shaking my head before we touched our gloves. I was a little dazed but felt okay. It was my ego that had taken the most damage after setting me up for a fall. The other fighter made sure that I was all right and Tony checked that I wasn't concussed. He cleared me to drive home. "That's boxing, kid."

    My adrenaline was flowing for a while afterwards, but as the sweat dried the pain increased. It felt as if my tooth was twisted and I debated whether to get it checked out. It was late, and most dental clinics were closed. As I was mulling over my options, the pain began to spread around the lower part of my face. My mouth was throbbing and tightening. I knew I couldn't sleep through that kind of pain, so I rang a clinic: no answer. I rang another with the same result. The pain was getting worse. I had one more number. This time the receptionist answered. "I'm sorry, sir, we're closing." I explained my situation. "How would you rate your pain out of ten? Nine? Okay, we might squeeze you in if you can be here in five minutes."

Still in a tracksuit, I jumped on my bike to get there before they closed. The toe-tapping dentist was waiting with her arms folded, shooting dirty looks at both me and the receptionist. I should have felt guilty about making them work a little longer, but the pain had become so intense that I didn't care. The dentist rushed me through, asked a few curt questions and took some X-rays. She left me reclining in the chair, confused and in pain. Ten minutes later, she returned to deliver a harder punch than anything I had taken that evening. "Your jaw appears to be broken. You may need to have it wired." Bedside manner wasn't her strong point. "You need to take these X-rays and go to the hospital. Go home first and get some clothes. It could be a long night." I couldn't even stammer a response.

A torrent of thoughts came flowing through my already throbbing head. I felt sick as I formed images of months ahead with no work, sport, travel or solid food. I wheeled my bike home in a daze and packed an overnight bag for a long night of waiting. After a few hours and X-rays in the hospital, they told me to come back a few days later when the inflammation had gone down. They would then assess if my jaw was misaligned enough to warrant wiring. I went home with a pocketful of painkillers and a head full of doubts; I tried not to indulge in either of them. The next morning, my face and neck were so swollen that I could barely open my mouth. Mentally, I was feeling far more tender, with lots of time and thoughts to kill without work to distract me. All I could do was wait. Hypothetical situations with a wired jaw bounced through my mind, twisting into tangled knots.

Back in a hospital waiting room a few days later, it was an anxious wait for my appointment. I stared into space with my arms folded, trying not to think too far forward. My name was called out and I was told to wait somewhere else before the doctor eventually sat down with me. Everything hung on the next few words. It felt like I was back in the ring, trapped in the corner with my head down, hoping for the bell or a towel to be thrown in. All I wanted was to get out of there to come back stronger. Then came the verdict: my jaw was fractured in three places. There would be no solid food or exercise of any sort for a while, but I didn't need to get my jaw wired. A sigh of relief. Physically, I needed time and patience to heal but mentally I felt weaker than ever. I was determined never to feel so vulnerable again.

Recovery: Sometimes the cure is the cause
Rawai Beach, Koh Samui, Thailand
June 2013

Verdant green flashes by as I ride down a narrow dirt path. My skin senses the changing temperature as I zip in and out of jungle shade, clouds of dust billowing behind me. The scooter hums and then putters as I ease off the accelerator to round a sharp corner before firing it up a steep incline. I park the bike, put my black half-shell helmet on the handlebar and pop my sunglasses inside. Later, I'll learn to put everything in the shade. I'm a beginner again and eager to get started. I had flown out the day before from Ireland to the island of Phuket, off the west coast of Thailand. I'll meet Angie in two weeks but right now I'm going to make use of my time to train hard. The familiar smell of stale sweat in the gym mixes with the heavy air of the surrounding green forest. I get ready, a little unsure of myself as I take in my surroundings. So much is the same and so much is different. Equipment like heavy bags, thick ropes and large tractor wheels lie all around the sides of the gym. In the middle there's a boxing ring, its high platform dominating the surrounding space. I dread the idea of stepping back into it, but the next two weeks will be about preparing myself to get back up there again. The training will be harder than anything I had ever done before.

I lie face-down on the ground, trying to loosen out my lower back. Three flights and almost twenty-four hours of travel still lingers. I try to look busy while I wait for my trainer. I don't know what he looks like but I'm expecting to meet a Thai flyweight, all muscle and sinew wrapped tightly around a small frame. Instead, I notice a large pair of dark-skinned bare feet stop in front of me. I crane my neck up from my prone position and see a powerfully-built, dark-featured man looming over me. When I stand up to shake his hand, he still towers over me. His grip is firm, and his eyes lock with mine. His movements are slow, deliberate and certain. This is a man who is very sure of himself. He speaks in halting English with a deep, low drawl. No words are wasted. "*Sawadee krap*, Brian. Now you skip." I don't delay.

It takes less than a minute for beads of sweat to gather and trickle. I wipe my hand back over my head – freshly shaved for the summer – but there's no relief from the heat. The tin roof of the gym only provides shade from the sun but there's no moving air. Next, I'm told to do press-ups and shadow-boxing for ten minutes. My trainer, Chai, comes over to have a look at my technique and give pointers on how to improve it. "Relax, too tense. Longer jab, longer. Punch down the middle. Chin down, shoulder up. Turn hips more." Individual attention doesn't leave room for sloppy habits. In boxing classes with big groups, the coaches didn't have time to monitor everyone's technique. Here, there is nowhere else to turn: get it right or do it again. There's so much to improve upon, but that's part of the reason why I travelled thousands of miles to be there.

The next exercise is pad-work, focusing on combinations of different punches like jabs, hooks and uppercuts. I put on an old pair of hefty fifteen-ounce gloves and try to follow Chai's instructions. My reactions and timing feel as thick and heavy as the mid-morning air. I mix up hooks with cross-punches. I jab or duck right when it should be left. When I do get them right, my punches make a dull thudding sound on the pads. Chai keep calling for more: two punches, four punches, six, eight, ten. Similar instructions and tips follow. I do my best to carry them out, but fatigue is dragging me down. My eyes sting from the sweat that streams down my face. I lose my concentration and mess up the combinations. It feels like my body and mind are separate and one can't keep up with the other.

We go for another round of cross-punches: "Three-four, five-six." Even before I get to the last one, Chai sees that I need a break. My vision is distorted with flickers and spots of light in the corners of my eyes. The humidity, heat and travel all get to me and I feel so dizzy and weak that I want to vomit. Chai notices and tells me to take my time to recover. I'm only wearing a light pair of shorts, but they are soaked with sweat that has rolled down my back. He barks a few words in Thai and another trainer brings over some iced water. Chai pours some down the back of my neck and the cold snaps me out of my dizzy spell. Chai tells me to take off my gloves and sip water. After a challenging hour, it feels good to have made it through.

About a minute or so later, Chai then calls out something that I don't quite catch at first; my mind is still fuzzy. I repeat the sentence a couple of times in my mind to catch the meaning. "Okay, now we spar, Brian." The words ring around my ears for a few moments. "Okay, now we spar." It still takes a few seconds to register with me. *I'm not ready. I just want to train, not spar. It's my first day. There's no headgear. I haven't signed up for this.* "Gloves on," he says. My mind wants to go from fight to flight, but Chai is telling me to glove up, not asking. My senses are so overwhelmed that it seems silly to question one more shock of many to my system. Chai is the owner of the gym and even though he speaks excellent Thai, he is German. This somehow makes him seem even bigger. My heart races but I try to think only of what I'm doing and not about the huge German deftly shadow-boxing in front of me. I start to glove up.

"Okay, box." We circle one another on the heavy gym mats next to the ring at the centre of the gym. My mind and body are tense: shoulders hunched, chest tight, breathing heavily. Although Chai has a strong upper body, his movements are loose and fluid. His hands keep a low guard, almost inviting me to try to punch over them. I direct a few hopeful jabs, but his nimble footwork and head movement mean they never get close to their target. As he skilfully evades my punches he sends back some of his own that skim across the top of my head. He is not connecting fully but just letting me know there are gaps in my defence. When I protect both sides, he sends a straight jab smacking against my forehead. When I guard my middle tightly, he clips me around the ear. Each lesson ends with a punch. Chai keeps repeating, "Relax, relax," in his deep Germanic drawl.

    I get to the point where I just want to hang on without getting hurt or making more of a fool of myself than I already have. I'm either too tense or too tired to follow the signals Chai is giving me. He tries to draw as much as he can from me without pushing me too far. He recognises the point at which I've nothing left to give and calls an end to the session. I had never experienced anything like the physical and mental intensity of that ninety minutes. Chai must have felt that he was in for a long two weeks, training me every day, but he never let it show. I slowly unwind as I take off my boxing wraps and flex my fingers to get them moving again. I feel sluggish as the humidity and fatigue begins to weigh heavily on my shoulders.

    Although I've made so many mistakes in the session, the sensation of physical and mental exhaustion makes me think that I've done something right. I'm dazed before midday but ready to come back for more. I thank Chai and wave goodbye to everyone else. Walking towards the scooter, I feel heat radiating from the seat. The helmet is too hot to put on, so I pour some water over it to cool it down. I pause for a while and take in the jungle view that spreads out behind the gym. A few deep breaths and I feel energised enough to ease the bike down the sharp hill that leads on to the dirt track. I'm shattered but I feel a smile spread across my face. I know then that I've come to the right place.

Mindset: Relax to allow room to improve

We are sparring again. I try to think of all the little instructions I've heard over the last four days: move, relax, load hips, stay loose, guard up, jab long, guard up, rotate, guard up! I've become more accustomed to the heat, but even though my body feels fresher my head is clogged with information. Whenever I punch with my right, I let my guard down on the left side. I'm repeating the same mistake that led me here in the first place. Chai has no qualms about exposing it. He isn't punching hard but it's enough to hurt. My nose stings, my eyes water or my head thuds every time he connects. All I can do is step back to shake it off and start again.

I must attack to defend myself, but my jabs are slow and predictable. Chai dominates the middle of the mat, his movements light, loose and evasive. For a big man, he doesn't give me much of a target to hit. He exposes only his left shoulder with his chin tucked neatly behind it. His head is turned down but the whites of his eyes peer out at me. They spot my punches before I even throw them. I try to find an opening but every time I push forward, I leave myself open and he clips the top of my head. The clunky heaviness of my movement is in marked contrast to his languid footwork. Neither of us is wearing headgear but he doesn't even have a mouth-guard. He doesn't need one. His open defence with his hands hanging low frustrate and mock me even more. I put in so much effort but seem to be getting nowhere. My whole body tightens with tension as I fire out hopeful punches that barrel through the humid air. He slips past them and jabs arrows in return.

"Relax, relax," Chai repeats, dragging out each of the vowel sounds. I'm being hit and told to relax at the same time, which annoys me even more. In my head, I'm shouting back: *Stop telling me to fucking relax!* I keep that voice where it is. I don't want the lesson, I want the answers, preferably without being hit on the head. I'm trying my hardest and I can't even get close to punching this big German. After four days, I seem to be making more mistakes than ever. Chai calls time on the session.

It's late afternoon and the day is growing a little cooler. The gym is empty, and we start chatting as we unravel the wraps on our hands. I had initially assumed that Chai came from a mixed German-Thai background, as he is quite dark and speaks the language fluently; however, he tells me he is German born and bred. His accommodation is a simple cabin right next to the gym. Christened as Ralph, reborn as Chai. I find out later that it's a common Thai nickname meaning 'victory.' He is so at ease with himself that I feel comfortable enough to tell him why I've come to Thailand. I tell him about breaking my jaw and admit my frustration at my lack of progress; particularly the fact that I'm still dropping my guard before punching. Why haven't I learned? Chai seems genuinely surprised by what I'm saying and by the emotion crackling in my voice. "Just four days you are here," he responds. He focuses on the positive aspects of what I'm doing and how far I have come in a brief time. It puts me in a more positive frame of mind that isn't clouded by emotion. "You need to relax, Brian." It finally gets through that it's my over-eagerness to get ahead which is blocking my progress. Like a rope frozen in winter, I cannot stretch myself any further until I loosen up. It's the same advice he has been giving since I arrived but now I'm ready to listen.

Direction: Review your progress

Later that evening I remind myself how thankful I should be for the chance to train and improve with someone like Chai. I don't want to let him down or waste his time, but there are so many little tweaks and techniques that it's difficult to remember them all. To help me remember them, I start scribbling a few notes, cues and sketches in the back of an old travel journal. Eventually my notes become more elaborate and descriptive as I jot down more about what I'm thinking and feeling. By the second week, it has become a habit to which I look forward each evening; sitting on the balcony of my rented apartment, going over my day with some Thai whisky on ice and chocolate on the side. Most evenings I keep writing until the mosquitoes arrive to send me inside.

Mindset: Knowing our weaknesses can make us stronger

Journal Entry: Leaning on Chai
Rawai Beach, Koh Samui, Thailand

I suppose I pride myself on my drive and resilience, so I was surprised that I felt so despondent after training on Wednesday. Chai only said a few words, but they were enough to give me a different perspective. Maybe I need to consider it brave to admit that I'm struggling. I can't become better if I can't see my weaknesses. When you trust someone, they will inevitably lift you up on the days you struggle. Chai has shown himself to be someone I can trust. Yet again, boxing training has shown me that it has no place for pride.

Progress: Sow what you want to grow

It's early morning in the boxing gym and no one is around. All I can hear is my own breath and the sounds of the jungle as I shadow box and then practice punches on the heavy bag: breaking down the little steps and repeating drills to commit them to muscle memory. Easy effort, strict on technique. I recall the cues from my notes: *drop left knee, turn right hip, whip the jab*. This slow, deliberate practice is like digging a channel through which water will flow. An hour later, the gym is still empty, and I slip away without being noticed.

Back in boxing gym late that day. "1, 2." Pop, pop. "1, 2, 1, 2." Pop, pop. Pop, pop. The sound of leather on leather snaps and cracks through the afternoon air as Chai calls the punches. I focus only on the whites of his eyes and the pads. I don't even think about the swipes he throws at me every few punches; I just duck under and come back for more. My mouth is shut. My ears are sharp. My mind is quiet. My eyes are wide behind my gloves. I try to connect to each moment as it happens, instinct over decision. Pop, pop. Pop, pop. "Okay, we spar now." It's our last sparring session so we step into the ring. I perch my camera on a scaffolding pole to record it, so I can watch it later. This time, I feel ready.

Direction: When you're lost, slow down and find a guide

<u>*Journal Entry: Fresh Perspective*</u>
Rawai Beach, Koh Samui, Thailand

When I watched the video of the sparring session this evening, it looked as if someone else was in there with Chai. Still no headgear, no footwear, but I looked different. My movement was free from the tension that had held it tight at the start. *I kept it simple today: relaxed but ready to attack and defend. Being more relaxed had a steadying effect. I wasn't wasting punches or energy trying to be better than I am. On Chai's advice, I switched my stance back and forth from orthodox to southpaw. When I started jabbing with my right hand, it corrected my old fault of dropping the guard protecting my chin. It gives me a different angle, a fresh way of moving. What hadn't worked going forward, worked in reverse.*

Chai has shown me that there are different ways to get ahead; some can mean going back, or going more slowly, but ultimately making progress. I hadn't recognised my early frustration as the 'dip' – the inevitable period during the learning process when initial enthusiasm fades as you realise how little you really know. Thinking that I should be better wasn't going to make me any better. Chai has taught me to work with things as they are instead of how I want them to be. A good coach sees the full picture, not just the steps or results we want to see as learners. Coming out swinging might land a big punch or two but that won't last for long. My mind and body need to work together to drive me forward. I'm not sure where I'll take my boxing from this point on, but I know I can take what I've learned with me.

Routine: Run early and make the day taste better

After my short stay in Thailand, I met up with Angie in Kuala Lumpur to fly onwards to South Korea where we would stay with my sister. Seoul's neon confusion was tinted with glimmers of nostalgia. Memories flooded back of a very different life that I had once lived there. Long-lost friends made for full days and fuller bellies, and a couple of weeks flashed by with some early mornings but more late nights. Our daily routine was as unpredictable as the Korean weather but, haphazard as our lives were while travelling, I nearly always managed to fit in some running. I can't say that it was enjoyable all the time, but I always felt better afterwards.

When we moved on to Bali, I did my best to avoid the humidity of an Asian summer and the heavy traffic on the roads by getting up in early morning darkness. Eventually, the heat and the honking of horns always caught me as the sun rose higher, but once I got out for a morning run the rest of the day tasted better. It gave a little direction to my day that I would complement with lazy afternoons sipping strong coffees or cold beers. Any day I didn't run, a hotel breakfast of fruit and coffee just gave me a sugar rush and subsequent crash, but after an early morning run it seemed to be exactly what my body needed. I also got to see secluded little pockets of local life which I cherished more than tourist sites: mothers washing clothes, families going to pray, children walking to school. Running was a way to experience a truer version of the world around me.

Progress: Sometimes the best way forward is the simplest

When Angie and I returned home after our summer in Asia, I thought about what I wanted to do next. I had stopped playing gaelic football five years previously, and during that time I'd had no focus to push me on a consistent basis. There had been a lot of movement as I went from one thing to another, but I wasn't excelling at anything. Soccer and boxing had been great, but there were too many factors outside my control: waterlogged pitches, cancelled matches, long journeys, terrible referees or crowded boxing gyms with ever-changing coaches of varying quality. Running was simplicity itself: gear, watch, house key and out the door. I had far more control of my training and had no one to blame but myself if training didn't go well. The changeable Irish weather was beyond my control, but I was more appreciative of Ireland's wet roads after Bali, where the game of 'chicken' seemed to be the common law of the land. Running and boxing over the summer had garnered enough momentum to get me to the middle of the hill, so I decided to keep running and see where it would take me.

CHAPTER 5: A RUNNING START

Race Report: Charleville Half-Marathon

It was my first race in twelve months. The previous year, after a summer of clean living in Morocco and nearly two months of training, I had run a personal best of 1:25:05. *Ah, but those five seconds.* That's how I learned my first rule of running: always double-knot. I missed out on breaking 1:25 because I had to stop to tie my laces. I felt I could beat that time as I had been consistently running for around two months and after the training in Thailand I was at my leanest weight since I'd been a teenager – I had dropped from around seventy-four kilograms to seventy (163 to 154 pounds). The obvious race target was to break 1:25. I'm not too sure at what point I developed the perverse concept of time so widespread among runners whereby seconds and minutes matter so much but breaking that 1:25 milestone became the focus of my training. Each run was judged on whether it was preparing me to break that time. '1:25' shone like neon lights in the back of my mind.

When race day came, I felt positive about reaching my target. I drove to the race with a friend, Leo, who was a member of a running club and had been running consistently for a few years. I was glad of his company and advice on the way. His race results indicated that he was a little ahead of me in terms of his development but was at the level to which I was aspiring. I decided I would try to stay with Leo for as long as I could, reckoning that he might drag me through the tough patches. Having trained so much on my own, I thought it would be enjoyable to run alongside someone I knew. In any case, I had forgotten my watch, so he would have to pace me.

We stuck with each other as the miles built up, but by the time we got to the halfway point I realised we were running at a much slower pace than I had thought: it was two minutes over an even split for 1:25. That might not seem like a lot, but it meant running the second half over four minutes faster than the first to meet my target. "We need to pick up pace here, Leo," I said. He shook his head in response but encouraged me to go ahead on my own. Making up the time was unlikely but possible; it was like chasing someone who was running at a similar pace but giving them a kilometre of a head-start. Even though I was annoyed at giving myself so much work to do for the second half, I was ready to take it on. I had nothing to lose.

With no watch to pull me back or push me forward, I just let go and ran. I remembered the second rule of running I had learned when I used to struggle to complete runs over an hour: *run what you can see.* If I wasn't running to the next mile-marker, I was running to the next runner. I kept passing people, so I knew I was making up for lost time. By mile eight (13 km), I had gone past around ten runners and with each mile I was passing several more. By mile ten (16 km), I still felt strong and confident. *Jesus, maybe I can do this.* I wanted to ask someone the time but kept pushing on instead. Pondering paces wasn't going get me a 'personal best'. I just had to give it everything for the last few miles. A burst of enthusiasm propelled me into mile eleven. There were no more runners ahead, so my only competition was the clock.

Mile twelve and the flow from earlier had quickly turned to fatigue. I was running on my own with only a few drags on the road to keep me company. My legs were heavy from the accumulated miles and my face was beginning to show it. My eyes burned in the morning cold, lips dotted with spittle, my mouth twisted in search of air: I was the ugly face of running. The last mile went back through the little country town of Charleville among locals ambling home after Mass. They clapped us along even though many of them had thick Sunday newspapers tucked under the crook of their arms. They lingered a while, but the promise of a breakfast of bacon and eggs wafted through the air and beckoned them homeward. Those little vignettes of daily life can be comforting but also serve as reminders of the lunacy of runners' Sunday morning pursuits. For a few fleeting moments, I dreamed of an easy start to the day with tea and rasher sandwiches: bacon on toast slathered with Bandon butter and tomato relish. My thoughts were trying to take me somewhere else, anywhere away from the pain.

Not much left now. My focus was back on the road and the last corner that loomed ahead. I kept my gaze on that sharp turn that would bring sight of the finish line and an end to the pain. There was a slight incline in the way, but I ignored the pleas from legs to make it all stop. Once I turned that corner, I managed a sprint, or at least it felt like one. My hamstrings burned in response, but I reassured myself that it was the quickest way to make the pain go away. I spotted the race clock at the side of the finishing area and knew that I was very close to breaking 1:25. I didn't care anymore; I just wanted to cross the line so that it could all be over. I gritted my teeth and closed my eyes for the last few strides. No graceful finish for me; instead I staggered like a crab to the side, bent over with my hands on my hips. For a few unsure moments I stayed doubled over, contemplating the benefits of vomiting.

 Once I was fully upright and no longer nauseous, my thoughts drifted to finishing times. I thought I was very close to breaking my target, but I couldn't be sure as I had crossed the starting line a few seconds behind the race clock. I would have to wait until later when the official chip times were confirmed. I caught up with Leo and Dinger before heading to the local hall, which had tables laden down with food. I really enjoyed the easy chat while devouring plates of sandwiches and cakes washed down by steaming cups of tea. Reliving the race eased our aches and pains and made me forget how tough I found it at the end. With enough time and tea, tough times almost always seem better. As we were leaving the hall, the provisional finishing times were pinned up on a wall. The results would be confirmed by text message later, but I decided to spare myself the wait. 1:24:56: four seconds under my target. Dinger had finished well ahead of me, but I thought, *that'll do, donkey, that'll do!* It almost felt better to run under my target by only four seconds than an ample cushion of time.

 What next? I wasn't too sure if I would continue running over the winter. I didn't think I could improve my time significantly and the next milestone would have been to break 1:20, which didn't seem possible. Returning to playing soccer was still something which appealed to me, maybe with a different team playing at a higher level. On the way back to my car, I changed my decision to opt out of buying a finisher's medal. My PB could be engraved on it for posterity and bragging rights: a reminder of when I'd been a runner. Later, I posted a rare social media update with my beer and pizza-laden plans for recovering from my

PB run. The complimentary messages were probably just another way for me to extend the adrenaline buzz from the morning; it's hard to let go of a good race.

Two beers later, after plenty of positive comments on my time, I received a text with my confirmed finishing time. It read: 1:25:00. I stared at the screen: 1:25:00. I hadn't broken it. Every time I blinked, I expected a different time in front of me, but it was still 1:25:00. I later read several online comments from annoyed runners about the difference between their provisional and confirmed times. I had visualised 1:25, and that's what I'd got. It felt like a punch in the gut. The medal gleaming in the corner and my online post glimmering on the computer screen mocked me even more. *Where did I lose those seconds? Why hadn't I paced the race more evenly? Why hadn't I worn a watch?* It's still the only race I've ever run in which there has been a difference between provisional and official finishing times. It was also the only time I had been sent a text of an official result of a race shorter than a marathon. Even now it doesn't seem believable to have finished on that exact time. However, those seconds left hanging in the air changed everything: instead of being the end of my running, they became the beginning.

Attitude: Enjoy the process

I had placed so much value on beating a time that anything else felt like a failure. I wouldn't let it go until I had beaten that time. Scouring websites for upcoming races, I found another half-marathon just two weeks later. It was ironic that this race was being held on my old university campus, where it had taken me a long time to learn anything. Limerick was a university that I loved but many lessons and lectures had been missed in my time there. I had chosen to study languages and computing, but I found the university environment stifling. It was only after spending a year abroad working and studying that my attitude changed. Living a language made much more sense to me than learning it for an exam. When I returned home I was more motivated and my exam grades vastly improved. When I started to enjoy the process, the results followed. I hadn't made that connection with running as I was still more motivated by beating times. It took another trip to Limerick for that lesson to sink in.

Race Report: University of Limerick Half-Marathon

Despite running only three half-marathons in three years, I was lining up for my fourth two weeks later. I was fixated on running 1:24. Even so, I felt a little guilty over dragging Angie out of bed on a Sunday morning. It was a four-hour round trip, all for the prospect of finding a few seconds. I kept telling myself and Angie that all I wanted to do was run 1:24 so that I didn't have to run any more races. If this race was going to be my last one for a while, then I wanted to make it count.

It was a little surreal to line up at the starting-point, which was directly across from the university library – a location in which I had rarely found myself as a student. The race course got stranger from there, with a bizarre detour at the beginning around an artificial soccer pitch to make up the full distance. As a further distraction, there were three races all going on at the same time: a ten-kilometre race, the half-marathon and a thirty-kilometre race. The course was flat by Irish standards, but it didn't seem to be designed for fast times with lots of sharp turns and corners. We also had to weave between walkers from the other races.

Even though I was determined to break my personal best, I also wanted to enjoy the race and take in the familiar surroundings that seemed so different in the bright light of a Sunday morning. I high-fived any outstretched little hands bravely supporting us along the way. In all my years there, I had never managed to greet a Sunday morning fit and fresh, but twelve years late was better than never.

After the first few kilometres, the field of runners began to thin out quickly. I was running between groups, well behind the leaders. Although I was running on my own, I tried to keep two runners, around a hundred metres in front of me, within my sight. One of them had a shaved head and a full red beard so was duly christened 'Beardy Monk.' The other was clad in Lycra, with a large bandana over slicked hair and tanned skin, so I named him 'Italian Gigolo.' Whatever happened, I said to myself, I would keep the Monk and the Gigolo within eyeshot. It was a straightforward guide as I didn't have a GPS watch. My strategy was to break up the race into two blocks of five miles, to be run close to my target pace, and then give it everything I had for the last three miles. *Respect the distance first, the race can wait.*

After five miles (eight km), I figured out that I was a little behind the target pace. I usually start slowly so wasn't too worried. I expected my legs to be able to pick up the pace for the second block. One of the reasons that I like races that last over half an hour, is that you have time to react. When you're ready to push the pace, you hope that you have the strength in your legs and lungs, but you often don't know until you try. On this occasion, I was working hard for every mile. The flow and ease that I had experienced for the same block two weeks beforehand were nowhere to be found. At each mile marker, I was trying to figure out if I was on pace but was too addled to do even simple calculations. It wasn't until I reached the round number of the tenth mile (sixteenth km) that I was able to accurately check my progress. I was behind pace. It's tough to realise that you need to make up time after putting down ten hard miles (sixteen km). My mind was struggling to lift my heavy legs. Maybe two half-marathons in a fortnight was too much to demand of my body. I felt my pace dropping and took a few moments to compose and steady myself. *Breathe. Scan body. Straighten back. Deep breath.* My thoughts took on a more positive spin. *At least I'm going to finish the distance. I'm not that far off the pace. Just give it everything.* My mind was willing me forward, but my legs weren't yet ready to follow.

Mile ten (sixteen km) took its toll on a long straight road with an incline that was probably only noticeable if you were running on it. Weaving around walkers added some extra strides and strain. My legs felt as if I were running on sand. I tried to quieten my mind by locking my gaze back on the Monk and the Gigolo, who were a little less than a hundred metres ahead of me. Mile eleven (eighteen km) looped back down the same incline that I had struggled to climb. It was the same road but a different side and a fresh perspective. I lifted my head and my legs loosened out. I noticed the distance to the Monk and the Gigolo was a little shorter. Either they were weakening, or I was growing stronger. In any case, I wasn't going to let the race end without taking them on. The walkers disappeared, and I gained more ground. Little wins mean a lot to a tired mind. With gritted teeth and furrowed brow, my field of vision narrowed down to the space between us. Trying to catch the Monk and the Gigolo was going to be a race between heaven and hell.

After twelve miles (nineteen km), I was close enough to hear their feet hit the ground. I was feeling pain but seeing the reward. When I saw the 'one mile to go' sign, I was close enough to hear the Monk panting and knew it was time to make my move. Within seconds I went from being a few strides behind him to a few ahead. I tried to keep my breathing smooth, wanting him to think I was floating even if I felt like I was sinking. If he thought I was tired, he might have countered and pushed the pace again.

The Gigolo was still a few steps ahead, but I just concentrated on trying to run whatever was left in me. We crossed the River Shannon over the 'Living Bridge,' which swayed as we pounded along. There was about half a mile left. I took my chance to push on past the Gigolo, in too much pain to appreciate the moment. Years of playing sport seemed to have given me a burst of pace to make the hard yards even when exhausted.

All I could see in front of me was chaos as runners and walkers of the three different distances all crossed paths at the finish. There were even some supporters crossing the course. I ran dead straight ahead, too tired for anything but tunnel vision: pains brings focus whether we like it or not. My mind was ringing with alarm bells from burning legs. Only the finish line could deliver silent relief, but then it got worse. Crossing the line exhausted, I assumed my usual end-of-race position: doubled over with a crablike shuffle to the side of the finishing area. My head, arms and torso all felt too heavy. Resting my hands on my knees, I added something new to my post-race repertoire by vomiting. As clichéd as it might sound, I knew then that I had literally nothing left. I had given it everything.

Later that evening, my time was confirmed: 1:24:56. In the petty world of runners' finishing times, those few seconds meant a lot. Surprisingly, once I had broken the time, something strange happened; it no longer mattered. Reaching a target showed I was starting to run towards my potential, but the qualities I had developed to get me there, were the real prize. The rush of racing times spiked and then faded, but the satisfaction from training and preparing for weeks was far deeper: the process was worth more than the results. Valuing race times above all else meant I was still being driven by an ego that wanted to be inflated, regardless of whether that was through running or soccer. It was only when I had achieved what I had wished for that I realised, it wasn't what I really wanted or needed.

I thought back to the previous race in Charleville, when I'd fallen short of my target. I recalled how I'd spent the second half of it gliding along in my own little cloud with no watch ticking through my mind. In between the dips and the struggles there were little moments that flowed with a lightness of being that lifted me higher for days afterwards. I'd had a taste and I wanted more.

CHAPTER 6: CONNECTING THE DOTS

Routine: Always find time and space to move

"You can't connect the dots looking forward; you can only connect them by looking backward." (Steve Jobs, Stanford Commencement Address, 2005)

Travel and my unreliable sense of direction always reminds me that the events in our lives often don't make sense, until we look back at them. My talent for getting lost means that I become intimately familiar with all the unfrequented side streets of any city I visit. It's frustrating at the beginning, but after a couple of days of wandering I begin to see how all the streets, alleys and avenues link up with each other. Clarity can emerge from confusion. The year I took up running coincided with a topsy-turvy six months that were chaotic and overwhelming at times, but I emerged with a greater sense of direction that has stayed with me ever since.

In the second half of that year, Angie and I moved between four different houses and lived out of boxes, bags and suitcases. We stayed in lots of spaces and places but none of them our own. One of the few constants through it all was running. It gave me room when there was none to be found. I didn't need a gym, a pool, or a bike. No matter where I was, my runners were always there, ready and waiting. Training had become about something else: I ran to clear my head, ran to feel better, ran to get some space. When I had long lists of jobs to be done, lacing up and going out made me feel that, at least, I was doing one thing right. Just six weeks after my last half-marathon, I was back for more. It became another dot in the right direction.

Race Report: Clontarf Half-Marathon

One last race for the year. I wanted to have one last thrill from racing before winter settled in. Longer races were few and far between in November, but I found one in Clontarf on the northside of Dublin. It made sense until the alarm went off at five a.m. in the pitch dark of a Sunday morning. Driving three hours with a tight hamstring and without a coffee further fuelled my doubts on the sense of it all. Caffeine was ordered on arrival, but I struggled to loosen out my left hamstring. While changing in the tight space in the back of the car, I silently cursed as I wrestled with a sock. *Bloody hamstring!* I hadn't eaten properly either. The race hadn't even started, and I felt like I was already trailing the pack. At least Angie was there with me; frustration and discomfort never seem quite so severe when someone else is enduring them alongside you. That morning, she shivered with the cold, her gloved hands cupping her mouth; I would have understood if she'd been cursing me under her breath.

Journal Entry: Angie

I'm grateful for the love and balance Angie gives me. She understands that I need to push myself but has softened my edges and taught me how to be a more rounded person.

Clontarf is an area of Dublin that feels like a seaside town. There's a wide, open promenade that hugs the shore and eventually sweeps into the wild dunes of north Dublin. The old red-bricked shops are hunched together in what looks like a bid to protect themselves from the winds that whip in from Dublin Bay. Near the starting line, many runners followed suit in little groups, turning their backs and bracing themselves against the November chill. Feeling a little flat, I wanted a quick boost of energy but had no gels or sweets. I asked another runner for one of their jelly sweets, something I hadn't done in at least thirty years. The little bit of sugar along with the caffeine from my coffee perked me up. We could have been at home enjoying our Sunday morning in bed but, even in the cold, I was happy to be there. I had to remind myself that I was lucky to be able to run in a beautiful part of Ireland which I had never visited before. Sometimes we just need an excuse to break our routine and go somewhere new, regardless of the elements. In any case, if we only went outside in good weather in Ireland, we wouldn't get to see much.

Some winter sun rewarded our Sunday morning endeavour as we lined up to begin. A gun sounded the start of the race and a battle with the sea breezes. The race route began on the grassy promenade and brought us along a road that skirted the sand dunes. I would love to say that I embraced the wildness of it all, but my ego was still chasing times. The first ten kilometres were officially timed and even though my first training programmes were all for that distance, I had never officially run a race. I couldn't resist the temptation of setting a decent 10km personal best.

I tried to keep up with a runner just in front of me. He was running with ease in his stride and a smile on his face.

His springy stride earned him the nickname 'Hoppy'. In contrast, my shoulders were hunched as my mind crunched paces and times. I laboured behind him for several kilometres, but he eventually bounced away from me. As I passed the 10km mark, I noticed the digital time at the last second. It flashed a time that didn't make sense: 38:07. My eyes were watering from the wind, so I looked back a second time; it was still thirty-eight minutes. I had tried to run under forty minutes on my own in ten km training and had never managed to do it. Now I was doing it near the halfway point of a longer run. It was encouraging but running has a habit of humbling you again without too much delay. My dose of humility was served up when the lead runners started back towards me on the looped course. It's inspiring to see people running at that speed, but it was almost like watching a different event run by an alien species. The beauty of running is that everyone has their own challenge within the same race and mine was about to get tougher.

Battle of Clontarf Part II: Quicksand and the magic mile

The tightness in my hamstring became worse as I reached mile eight (eleven km). Driving for three and a half hours wasn't ideal preparation for a race and I hadn't been able to stretch or loosen it out enough in the warm-up. It wasn't a tweak or a twinge but more like a hard knot that got hotter as the race went on. To make matters worse, the course terrain changed. We merged onto Clontarf beach, passing through a soft patch of sand before being directed to firmer sand closer to shore. My hamstring became much worse on the heavy surface. The soft sands offered up an excuse to drop out. There was enough truth in all my excuses to make them sound reasonable. *You could damage your hamstring more. You already have a 1:24 time, what's the point in doing another one? It's the last race of the season, just enjoy it.* The sand beneath my feet was weighing heavier on my mind than my legs.

As I looked out on to the Irish Sea, the harsh breeze whipped around my ears. It made my nose and eyes water but snapped me out of my mental fuzz. I leaned into the wind, not thinking about style or stride but only of steps. *You can't drop out; it's too far to walk back. Angie would have to wait longer in the cold. You paid money and drove over three hours to do this.* Squinting ahead, I was surprised to see Hoppy was only around a hundred metres ahead of me. Now I had a new focus. Thoughts of my hamstring, the sand or the wind were all swept to one side; everything narrowed down to a target on his back. *Shut up and lean in.* Ignoring the wind blasting against my face, I imagined there was a rope tied between us and that I couldn't let Hoppy get any further than the length of it. I visualised dragging myself forward with my arms from the front and my legs from the back. I inched my way along that rope.

After a few minutes, I realised I was not only staying within the same distance but was closing in on Hoppy. It gave me strength where earlier there was none. Heavy sands might not have suited his style or maybe summer running on beaches had readied me for this very mile. I was close enough to see his face as we headed towards the last turn out of the beach. He was suffering as I had earlier. We turned up towards the pier; the sand became tarmac and I passed him out. I wanted to thank him for bringing me that far, but I kept it to myself; he had his own race to run. I felt a surge of energy at having achieved a goal that had seemed so out of reach just minutes before. The same body and mind that had almost given in, now pushed me forward. Fickle and strong all in one mile. In terms of developing my mental strength, that was probably the most important mile I've ever run.

I tried to redirect my gaze to another runner, but the next bunch was much too far ahead to catch at this stage of the race. Then I became conscious of a chasing pack behind me as the course spilled out onto an open grass promenade. It was hard not to imagine them working as a pack to gain ground on me. I couldn't tell if they were making progress or not, but my mind was drifting back instead of looking forward. It was much easier to chase than be chased; now I was the one with a target on my back. Hoppy had kept me focused on the only marker that mattered: running the yards in front of me. I was wishing, wanting and reaching for the finishing line far too early.

I told myself not to turn around. *Don't give them strength. Focus on your own run.* I just kept hanging on until I could finally see the finishing line. I always found a little more energy when it was in sight; same running, different mindset. I crossed the line and stayed steady on my feet. Maybe it was too cold for my usual theatrics or maybe I was getting stronger. Once I'd had my post-race hug from Angie, I quickly threw on some clothes to ward off the chill. There was a huge pot of soup bubbling up a warm welcome for the runners who gathered in clusters around it. Their cups were raised high so that the steam could warm their faces in between sips of the thick liquid. It had a warmth that only tired, cold bodies can truly appreciate. Just as we were about to head back to the car, a tall, lean runner caught me by the elbow. "Jaysus," he said, "'twas you I was trying to catch for the last two miles. Feck ya anyway, you stayed that bit ahead. 1:22, was it? Great running."

Battle of Clontarf Part III

Driving back down afterwards felt like another test of endurance as my left hamstring tightened up even more. By the time we arrived home, I was looking forward to stretching my leg on a bar stool. We met up with a few friends in a pub aptly named 'The Idle Hour'. On hearing that I had run a half-marathon earlier that day, someone in the group whom I hadn't met before, Paul, asked me my finishing time. People seem to feel duty-bound to ask this question of runners. I usually keep the details to a minimum to avoid the glaze that can wash over people's eyes.

Admittedly, when I replied "1:22" I felt far too satisfied with myself. I immediately drank a sizeable gulp of stout which could have been construed as dramatic effect but was more to dampen my burning ego. As I savoured the mouthful, the group were quick to offer praise. People are always genuine in their compliments even if they can't judge whether a time is particularly competitive or not. Sometimes there can be an over-exaltation of effort as if it's something only a few people can do. "I could never do that" or "I could never run so far or so fast" were comments that I was beginning to hear when people asked about my running. Someone said that Paul was a runner, so I was glad to know that any running talk wouldn't bore him at least. When he mentioned that his last race had been a marathon, runner's curiosity meant I eventually asked him his finishing time. I don't know what kind of time I was expecting but it wasn't 2:42. *How was that possible? Double the distance at a faster pace.* I gulped my pint again. "Jesus, I could never do that."

Challenges: Take them one at time

After Clontarf, a long period of recovery camouflaged a lazy reluctance to get out and train on cold winter days. With no target race on the horizon, my training was haphazard and heading nowhere in particular. I needed a challenge to snap me out of my post-race funk, so I came up with my own: *run further than I ever have before.* It wasn't going to be that far – around fifteen miles or twenty-four kilometres – but enough to get body and mind firing again.

On a cold December morning, I set off on my own with an i-pod to track my pace and distance. The longer distance should have meant running easy and forgetting about speed but every time I heard my splits, my ego kept driving up the pace. *This is too slow. I'm better than this.* Expecting just to pick up my running based on my last race, I hadn't factored in the lazy weeks since Clontarf. The pace shouldn't have mattered. I had forgotten what I had set out to do: run further than ever before. I was trying to push my endurance but was weighing myself down by adding pace. By the time I'd covered ten miles on rolling West Cork roads, I wanted no more. I had arranged to meet Angie at the far side of the seaside town of Clonakilty but contemplated flagging her down as she drove past. Fate saved me the ignominy of doing so but still had a good laugh at my expense.

Struggling on for another mile or two and I made it to the edge of the town. However, I couldn't get through to the road to Inchydoney beach, our prearranged meeting point. I had completely forgotten that the route would be blocked for a local marathon. As I stood near the finish line with my hands on my hips, part of me was relieved that the run was over but the rest of me was cranky because I couldn't think how to meet Angie. A race steward seemed to have pity and gave me a bottle of water. I absentmindedly mumbled my thanks before ambling back up towards a petrol station to ask for the use of a phone. Entering the shop, I was confused to hear compliments being given in my direction. "Well done! Fair play to ya." Everyone had justifiably assumed that I had just run a marathon; I disappointed them all with my embarrassed explanation and asked to use a phone. As I gulped my complimentary water, a phone was begrudgingly handed over.

After arranging to meet Angie, I ran a gauntlet of well-wishers as I walked back down towards the town. "Congratulations! Jaysus, you're looking fierce fresh." I said nothing this time and just smiled like a simpleton. Luckily Angie picked me up soon afterwards and we made a short drive out to a little pub in the nearby village of Ring. It was much quieter; no runners having arrived at that stage. The waiter came over. "Janey Mac, you must be one of the quick ones! Extra spuds for you!" Angie began to giggle when she saw the look on my face. "Ah, well - actually I – ah, yeah, thanks, and maybe a few chips as well." I promised myself that I would finish the run another day but take on only one challenge next time. Then I ate my extra spuds.

Mindset: Be open to inspiration

That December, after my shortened long run, I started to think about my next running goal. I wanted a challenge that would provide me with enough enthusiasm and momentum to bring me into the new year. I thought back to my conversation with Paul in the pub. He'd been almost dismissive of the demands of marathon training. "It's still just running, a bit more and a bit longer." Most of all, he was positive and encouraging. His enthusiasm and casual demeanour - along with the pints of stout - had made a marathon sound possible. "Just go for it," were his parting words. I didn't make any decision that evening but a seed was sown that at any other time in my life wouldn't have found fertile ground.

It had been twenty-five years since I had seen my parents run, so I had almost forgotten they had both run marathons around the four-hour mark. It was easy to remember Dad as an athlete, but Mum had only a passing interest in sport unless we were involved and never really spoke about running. Determination, however, was not something she lacked. At one point, she was taking care of five of us under the age of ten. When we were a little older, she went back to nursing night-shifts. When she wasn't working or taking care of us, she was always busy cleaning, cooking or fixing things around the house. Always there whenever we needed her, yet she still found the time and energy to train for three marathons. I never thought about it growing up but all the inspiration I ever needed had been right there beside me.

Earlier that year, Angie and I had visited the grave of the poet W.B. Yeats while driving around the west of

Ireland. Near his grave in Sligo, one of his poems is inscribed into the ground: *He Wishes For the Cloths of Heaven.* As I read the words laid out before my feet, one of the lines jumped out for both its rhythm and my interpretation of it: *The blue and the dim and the dark cloths of night and light and the half-light.* It made me think of my own dimmed potential. There had been days in the sun, but most of the time I had let myself happily drift along in the dim half-light. It was time to step out of the shadows.

CHAPTER 7: FINDING A BETTER WAY

Routine: The perfect plan is the one that works for you

There it was, staring back at me from the front page of my journal: my running goal for the year. I felt a knot tighten deep in my chest as I read over the words once again. They simply said, 'Run a sub-3-hour marathon.' If I wanted a challenge, this was it. It was intimidating but still achievable. Fear gave way to excitement as I saw more possibilities than problems with stepping up my training for the next five months. Whenever I feel that kind of steady energy, like a water diviner on the cusp of finding a fresh source, I know that I'm on the right track.

Despite my initial enthusiasm, my motivation was soon diluted by the spirit of Christmas. Without a fixed structure or routine, it was too easy to make excuses not to train. Everything could start again in the New Year. I had been researching a variety of different running programmes for a while but had failed to find one that suited me. There seemed to be so many essentials to consider: weekly miles and weekly sessions, long runs and 'tempo' runs, speed and strength sessions, paces, bases and tapers. I would decide on one approach but then change my mind after reading criticism of it somewhere else. I wanted to be confident that I had the best programme possible but the idea of having a perfect plan was keeping me rooted to the spot. I was filling my head with so much information that I couldn't possibly put it all into practice.

As Christmas Day approached, I felt an urgency to define some sort of programme. I decided to switch my criteria to finding a running programme that worked best for me rather than 'the best' running programme. Eventually I chose to stick to what I knew, a version of the half-marathon programme. I had put the marathon on a pedestal and made it out to be something very different to what I was already doing. It's still running; just a little more and a little longer. Sometimes we need a bit of healthy disrespect to just go ahead and do something. The best time to start was there and then. I decided I would get up early the next morning to try out one of the speed sessions.

Mindset: Tomorrow is always a fresh start

It was still freezing outside as the day was just beginning to brighten. Most roads had icy patches, so I had driven to a trail that was frozen but firm underfoot. A cloud of fog hovered over the meandering river beside me. Once I hopped out of the car, I started jogging straight away, swinging my arms to warm up. The world around me was covered in a blanket of frost and the ground crunched beneath my feet. Whenever I take on a new challenge, I get a sense of looking at myself from above and asking myself: *Am I mad?* On a very frosty Christmas morning, I pondered that same question. I imagined the saner majority of the country to be either nestled in bed or being dragged out of it to open long-awaited presents. I couldn't come up with a particularly solid defence of my sanity and even less so once I started the speed session. The repetitions were far tougher than I had expected with short recovery periods in between (3 x mile/1600m @ 5:40 mile/3:31 km pace with 400 m jog recovery). Billowing clouds of breath betrayed my struggle to get ready for the next rep. My mind was quietened, thinking only of running and resting. The target paces were much too fast for my winter-heavy legs, but that morning was about starting anew.

After my last repetition I jogged slowly along the high river bank, just about able to keep up with the slow flow of the river. All was quiet, and I felt that I had taken my chance to get ahead of the world that morning. My thoughts were turning to coffee and eggs as another runner emerged around the corner. We shared the embarrassed look of two people catching each other skipping Mass, but also exchanged the runner's knowing nod. We had our own way to worship the world around us.

Routine: Take the time to learn how to do things right

I wish I could say that Christmas morning launched a purposeful new year but life in the form of 'to-do' lists seemed to wedge running out of the way for a while. The holidays were spent dashing around trying to get our new home sorted before our Christmas holidays finished. As I rushed through one job, I would be thinking about the next one to cross off the list. It was never-ending, with each task rolling into another. A nine-hour round trip to IKEA became a microcosm of my mood that January: cranky, confused and eager to get the job over with. Late one night, in my haste to assemble a wardrobe that had remained in its box for several days, I ended up putting a sizeable dent in a shelf with a hammer. A stream of expletives quickly followed but the hole remained. Jobs were getting done but at a pace that led to mistakes. Everything that I was doing needed to be done, but it was more important to get them done right. This house was our home and the wardrobe, complete with hole, would be ours for years to come. We weren't going to be moving on again in a few months. I decided to take my time finishing the wardrobe before rewarding myself with a cold beer. After a second one, I began to see the dent in a new light. It would act as a reminder that it was more important to take the time to do things properly. My hammer was retired for a few days and I took out my runners in preparation for the next morning. It was time to start running again.

Routine: Prioritise and value your time

Looking over my training programme, the same old question popped up: *Why?* Why was I was committing so much time and effort into training for a single event? I still wasn't sure if I had the right answer. Checking it off a 'bucket list' would have been the convenient reply, but that wasn't my motivation. The marathon itself wasn't even my motivation; it was the training. It helped me harness and value my energy. When I had an abundance of time, I valued it less and frittered it away. When it was scarce, I had to prioritise what matters most to me. If I wanted to spend time with Angie, have a full-time job and work on our home, I knew I had to either get up early to run or go straight after work. If I didn't run at those times, I wouldn't run at all. Instead of making life more complicated, it made it simpler: train or do something more important. If I wasn't selecting one of those options, I wasn't using my time well.

The running programme I had chosen was also about making the best use of my time. It's not the kind of programme I would follow now, but at the time I wasn't ready to commit to doing high-mileage. I had never clocked up more than twenty miles (32 km) in a week and

I didn't want to starting running six days a week just to add on more miles. I also enjoyed cross-training as I felt it kept me fresher for running. The FIRST 'run less, run faster' programme was the most time-efficient and varied one I could find. It had only three runs a week and two cross-training sessions. The weekly distance ranged from twenty-five miles (40 km) to a maximum of only thirty-two miles or just over fifty kilometres. Despite the low mileage, the programme wasn't easy.

Each run had a specific aim: speed, speed endurance and endurance. It included five '20-milers' and the runs were supplemented by forty-minute sessions of intense aerobic cross-training twice a week. The training paces were very challenging so there were two rest days built in to help recovery. There were very few accounts of anyone using the programme to run a sub-3-hour marathon, so the only evidence that convinced me that the programme could work was the fact that I had already used versions of it effectively for half-marathons. The programme suited me because I liked running at faster paces and enjoyed spinning or rowing to vary my training. Knowing that each part of the programme was demanding also focused my time and attention. Once I decided on the programme, every session was reassuringly laid out before me with the required paces and distances. Seeing the next five months of training so clearly mapped out made me wonder why I didn't put more thought into other areas of my life outside of running. What was the guide for the rest of my life? Two small backpacks and three house moves had already been pointing us in the right direction.

PART IV: GETTING BETTER – LIVING WELL

CHAPTER 8: LIVING PLAN

Living Well: Find the filter for your essentials

I was trying to bring more structure to my running, so surely it made sense to put a similar amount of effort into organising other parts of my life. Around the same time of the year that I decided on a training programme with a stripped-back simplicity, I found myself scratching my head and wondering why I was in a room full of possessions that I didn't want or need. That summer, we had travelled for two months with only hand luggage to save the time, hassle and money involved in checking in bags for several internal flights. When we packed our bags, we had to ask ourselves: *Do I really need this? Will it fit in the bag?* Having less made us more mindful of everything we owned, and we surprised ourselves by how little we really needed. It was a little puzzling, therefore, just a few months later to be in a room so laden down with stuff that I couldn't even begin to pick out what I really needed.

By November of that year, we had moved between three houses in five months with one more move to go. I just seemed to be carrying carloads of our stuff from one place to another. Here I was again in a room that was full of bursting backpacks, black plastic bin bags and brown cardboard boxes. They were all making valiant but inadequate efforts to contain our hastily-packed possessions. It was overwhelming to even think about sorting everything out. The quickest option was just to cram everything back in and leave the head-scratching for another day, but I was sure there had to be a better way to manage our things. I decided the best approach was to take a long coffee break.

In the midst of procrastination and a second coffee, I started reading accounts of something called 'Minimalism,' which described how people had simplified their lives by ruthlessly culling their possessions to the essentials. We had already done something similar while travelling and it had made it so much easier than carrying around cumbersome suitcases or backpacks. Surely, I thought, we could do something similar to make our house-move easier.

The room was divided into two sides: things to keep or donate, using a filter of *need, choice or enjoyment*. I had to stop keeping things 'just in case' I ever needed them. If I hadn't needed something in the previous twelve, or even six, months, would I ever need it? If I really appreciated or enjoyed something else such as a book, piece of art or memento, I held on to them. I kept items for which I had no alternative. For example, I didn't need my kettle-bell weights or use them every day, but I didn't have a convenient alternative. If I had several similar items, I would choose the ones I really wanted. Lots of clothes were donated to charity with this filter in mind. It was slow at the beginning, but the charity bags soon filled up. Having a template was the key to whittling down those items to be kept. If I caught myself holding onto something purely because I knew how much I'd paid for it, I quickly defaulted to the filter of *need, choice or enjoyment*. By the time I was finished, nearly everything I owned was a favourite item. Decluttering cleared the way for me to see the things that I valued most.

Living Well: Add value by taking away

Minimising my possessions made me consider how I was spending my money and my time. Going through all my clothes, I was surprised at how little I had worn some items of clothing. It stung a little to remember how expensive some of them had been. The message that price tags didn't equate to worth was one which was reinforced several times. In fact, getting rid of some of my possessions made me more content than owning them. They had filled space but hadn't added value. I had been working hard for several years in exchange for a payslip that I spent too easily, giving money a higher value than my time. I was wasting money but at least I could make more; I could never get time back.

An empty house was a clean slate and a chance to only bring the things that added value to the house. To begin with, we had hardly any furniture: two chairs, a folding table, a sofa-bed and little else. There was a small table-top gas stove in the kitchen but no fridge. We happily survived by cooking simple meals and keeping our beers cold outside. We possessed very little but had everything we needed. It all felt intimate, cosy and very much ours. It reminded me of my family home when the electricity went out and everyone sat around playing card games and arguing in candlelight. We wondered why we didn't do it more often but when the lights and TV flicked back on, we all scattered once again. I still remember those family chats and squabbles in the dark, but I don't remember anything about what we did when the lights came back on. In a similar way, once the New Year dawned I charged off with a long list of jobs and tradesmen to call. They all took up too much time and importance. I was distracted and scattered as training was pushed to the bottom of the list.

When pressure was put on my time, I lost sight of what was important to me. I felt grateful to have so many strong threads in my life at home and at work, but I couldn't see how successful I was at binding all those roles together. Was I loose and frayed, spiralling out in lots of different directions? Would I just unravel whenever life pulled a little harder? Even on the days that I didn't feel like running, I nearly always stuck to the programme, but I couldn't say the same for the rest of my life. Decluttering my possessions was the starting point to seeing things more clearly and finding a plan for living.

CHAPTER 9: LIVING THE WAY

Focus: Focus on what you can control

On a mountain-biking trip with friends, I once gravely overestimated the nutritional value of tea and cereal as sustenance for cycling over rough terrain in the Ballyhoura mountains between Cork and Limerick. Towards the end of the bike-ride, I was shivering from the cold and rain and trailing the rest of the lads. As I was grinding the gears over the greasy surface of a wooden walkway, the wheels of the bike slipped out from under me, sending me crashing to the ground. Even though I was a little rattled and my hands were shaking from a lack of energy, I got back on the saddle and kept going; I just wanted to get to the end. The thought of a fry-up was the only thing keeping me going, but first I had to negotiate a wooden swing-bridge. It had no protection on the sides so there was no hiding the murkiness that lay beneath. I glanced over one side at the dark, boggy ground and thought to myself, *I would hate to end up down there.* Where my thoughts went, my body followed. I tipped over like a falling tree, arse first, into black Irish bog land.

I was stunned for a few moments before the unique properties of an Irish bog kicked in. The clawing earth had a distinct property of cold, wet blackness that went right to my bones. It can preserve bodies for thousands of years and freeze mountain bikers in seconds. Lying there on my side with my legs neatly locked around the bike, I must have looked like some hellish version of a mermaid on the rocks. Falls are commonplace in mountain biking but are usually of a more dashing and daring nature; mine was more like slow-motion comedy. Once the stream of expletives had come and gone, I floundered my way out and free-wheeled to the finishing point. At least the bike was the only witness.

By the time I got to the end of the trail, my friends were clean, fed and more than ready to amuse themselves at how I had earned my extra coating of mud. It took a hot shower and a lot of food for me to see the funny side. For the rest of the morning, whenever I went to the bathroom – colloquially known as the bog – my helpful friends warned me not to fall in. On the journey back home, my friend 'Bull', who had derived much joy from my trip to the bog, offered a little piece of advice that stuck with me long after the mud was gone. "Keep your eyes on the path ahead. Don't be looking where you don't want to go." It was meant as a tip for mountain-biking, but one I remembered when I later started to read more about improving my mindset.

Mindset: Find a blueprint for success

When I was reading about the minimalist approach to living, I kept seeing references to a philosophy called Stoicism. I had always dismissed philosophy as a theoretical pursuit that raised more questions than answers. I didn't see how it could benefit me in practice. However, two blogs by people whose thoughts I enjoyed reading – Tim Ferriss and Mr. Money Mustache – extolled the virtues of implementing this practical philosophy into daily life so I decided to look a little deeper.

My preconceptions of Stoicism were based on the adjective 'stoic', which has been hijacked by modern English to mean impassive or emotionless. Even with just a little reading, it became clear that the philosophy of Stoicism is about trying to live the best version of our true selves every day in a way that is thoughtful, brave and honest. My basic understanding of Stoicism at that point could have been summarised by the first few lines of the Christian 'serenity prayer', which was written two thousand years after the founding of the Greek and Roman philosophy: *Grant me the serenity to accept the things I cannot change, courage to change the things I can and wisdom to know the difference.* Instead of cribbing or crying, a Stoic does what they can to help themselves or others. Stoicism isn't about being unemotional but about doing the best we can in whatever situation we find ourselves.

The men who wrote about Stoicism didn't just think or talk about it, they used it every day to better themselves. The three Stoics I enjoyed reading most were three men who had come from very different backgrounds: Epictetus, Marcus Aurelius and Seneca. Epictetus was a crippled slave who had been allowed by his master to study philosophy, and when he was later freed, founded a philosophical school. He lived very simply and saw philosophy as way of living rather than a theoretical pursuit. He didn't even write books; instead, a student published his lectures. The circumstances of Marcus Aurelius' life were very different: as leader of the Roman empire, he was one of the most powerful men in the world at that time. I had only been aware of him from his portrayal in the film, *Gladiator,* as the adopted father of the general, Maximus. His books were his personal journals where he wrote about his thoughts on how to better his life. They were insights into the mind of an emperor who struggled like everyone else with anxiety, focus and self-discipline. Seneca's career was more varied in that he had tutored a future emperor in his younger years and later became one of the wealthiest men in the world through business and politics. Despite his riches, he wrote about living in a way that didn't need or seek wealth.

One of Seneca's books, *Letters from a Stoic*, immediately connected with me. Even just reading a few lines on the very first page from the first chapter, *On Saving Time*, made an immediate impact. I didn't need to read much to see how I could apply it to benefit my daily choices. It is a philosophy which encourages practice, and that's what I started to do.

Mindset: Remember what is in your control

Journal Entry: What is really under my control?
January 2014

One of the tenets of Stoicism is that we control only what we think and the way in which we try to behave. Our decisions on how to live in the present will decide our future. Choosing how we eat, sleep, think, behave and exercise is what really matters. Our bodies are vessels which carry us around but don't necessarily co-operate with our minds all the time. If we suffer injury, illness or exhaustion, the greatest will in the world may not be enough to propel us forward. Ultimately, we have little control over our bodies, which will age over time no matter what we do. What we do control is the way we decide to live.

Alcohol: Don't let today take from tomorrow

Live in the moment, just as it says on the motivational posters, summed up my lifestyle after I stopped playing football. If I wanted to do something or go somewhere, I just did it without too much thought or reflection as there were no upcoming matches or training sessions to consider. In the same way, whenever I saw clothes that I liked, I bought them. My nature was to live 'off the cuff' and I thought that life should be enjoyed like nights out with friends: spontaneous and unplanned. If I wanted to go out on a weeknight for a few drinks as well as the weekend, I did. No doubt I questioned my habits on many wasted Sunday mornings, but the easy answer was that *you're only young once.* Over time I was sure that convenient excuse would change to, *you only live once.* As much as I enjoyed those nights that once seemed so spontaneous, they became part of a cycle that was repeated every week. I never peered through the looking-glass long enough to ask too many questions as everyone else around me was doing the same.

Maturity could wait for another day, but the hangovers never did. They became longer and more intense, leaving me sluggish and dulled for days. A few days of clarity would follow before the cycle started all over again. My beer-glass tinted view of the world gave me the illusion of freedom, but I was aimlessly wandering back to the same place every time. Once I made it clear that I still wanted to get better, it forced me to make better decisions on when, and how much, to drink. Every so often, I still drink too much but it serves to remind me why I try not to do so, too often.

Routine: Have a morning routine

"Why then am I dissatisfied if I am going to do the things for which I exist and for which I was brought into the world? Or have I been made for this, to lie in the bedclothes and keep myself warm?" (Marcus Aurelius, Meditations, 5.1)

Regardless of my age or location I used to try stay in bed as late as I could, whether it was before school, college or work. Bashing the snooze button was a means to delay the day by another few minutes. For most of my adult years, weekend mornings were spent hiding from hangovers under the covers. When I lived in South Korea in my early twenties, nights-out didn't finish until early morning and on many occasions, I dozed well past my subway stop. There is nothing quite so sobering as starting awake in a subway carriage full of Koreans on their way to work. I never mastered their seemingly genetic gift for awakening from a deep sleep and neatly shuffling out of the carriage just in time for their chosen stop. Instead I would awake panic-stricken with my head swivelling like a startled meerkat. It would take me a while to ascertain my whereabouts, but invariably I would be crushed by the realisation that I was heading towards the end of the subway line. I became very familiar with that green line during my time there. Since then, there had been a few isolated incidents of enthusiasm when I'd attempted early morning runs but they soon reassured me of the wisdom of sleeping in. I reasoned that I just wasn't a morning person. That was the story I told myself, and I didn't think I could change it. However, Stoicism was telling me that one of the few things I could control were my thoughts. If I could change the story I was telling myself, I could start living a better life. Running was going to be the means to prove it.

At the age of thirty-four, as my career had progressed, my workdays had become busier and more intense. Different parts of my life were always coming up with something extra to be done. There seemed to be very little time left over at the end of each day and there definitely didn't seem to be much space to add marathon training. *How do you find space when there appears to be none?* It was like adding something to a suitcase that was already nearly full; it was possible, but it would take a lot of moving things around. My usual time to run was in the evening but that meant I had to get through the rest of the day first. If something came up, training would have to be pushed to the next day. Instead of trying to chase time, I decided to try to take more control of my days and make time: early morning was the obvious place to start.

My habit of thumping the snooze button not only shortened my day but it would leave me feeling groggier and less rested. After some trial and error, I realised that I naturally woke at 6:30 a.m. and felt fresher if I got out of bed at that time rather than sleeping until later. I started pushing myself out of bed at 6:30 a.m. to do some light stretching and then eventually some easy yoga. I was surprised by how much I enjoyed having that extra time and space before work in the morning.

Once I'd become more accustomed to getting up earlier over the course of a couple of weeks, I added in a few easy runs to get used to the shock of exercising early. When I didn't spontaneously combust, I decided to step up to running some tempo sessions. They were much more challenging, but I always felt happy to have a session completed before my day had even started. There was never any time to bask in satisfaction as I then had to get my working day started. Later in the day, however, I was paid back with interest. I had more time and headspace to focus on my other priorities. I was doing more yet feeling better. Once I had experienced these benefits, I started to get up at the same time even on the weekends. I wanted to make it a daily habit rather than something I chose to do on some mornings but not others. The less mental energy I spent deciding whether to get up or not, the more likely I was to do it. If I left any room for indecision, my sleep-addled brain would take advantage and offer me several perfectly valid excuses to stay in my warm bed. It took me a while to learn how to silence those voices.

Motivation: Be ready for excuses

> *"Do not dwell on what you do not have but consider what you do have and select the best, then reflect how eagerly they would have been sought had you never had them." (Marcus Aurelius, Meditations, 7.27)*

No philosophy in the world can stop you from hearing the rain pattering against your bedroom window and the wind howling outside. That's when my weaker self likes to put a supportive arm and warm blanket over my shoulders and give me all the excuses I'm waiting to hear. *Run later when it's not raining or dark or cold* or *better to rest than run this morning.* There were mornings when I took up one of those tempting offers but later I would resent that evening run, hanging over me all day. Some mornings, I would trick myself out of bed by promising myself that I only had to run for ten minutes. Once I was out of bed, I always completed a full session. My imagination was skilled in making the weather seem worse than the reality, but I was becoming better at not giving into it.

Other days, it takes a stronger voice to quieten my mind and it's one that I'm not always ready to use or able to hear. Indeed, it's one to keep in reserve unless we really need it. It's a Stoic technique called *premeditatio malorum* – its more modern form is 'negative visualisation' – which is intended to foster positive action by considering something being taken from us. When we are sick, we value nothing more than our health; we would give anything to feel better again. Even something as relatively straightforward as a migraine, upset stomach or torn hamstring can quickly become the bane of our lives. But why do we often only value what we have when it is taken away? Negative visualisation encourages this appreciation without the need for loss. Imagining what it would be like to be unable to run reminds me that it's a gift to be healthy. If a day arrives when I cannot run ever again, what would I say looking back at myself lazing in bed? What would I give to have that strength back in my legs again? That could happen next week or in twenty years' time but all I can do now is make the best of what I have.

Now when I set that alarm for 6:30 a.m., I sometimes remind myself that, no matter how bad the weather might be the next day, I should be grateful to be able to put my two feet out of bed, pick up my running gear, get ready and run out into the morning. And when that alarm sounds, that's exactly what I do.

CHAPTER 10: TRAINING FOR SPEED

Consistency: Focus on the process not the goal

"The wise man regards the reason for all his actions, but not the results. The beginning is in our own power; fortune decides the issue, but I do not allow her to pass sentence upon myself." (Seneca, Moral Letters to Lucius, 14.16)

As I rounded each lap of the track, the digits on my watch seemed to be telling me lies. I was panting while squinting at a time that showed I wasn't anywhere near my target paces for the speed session. I thought I must have miscalculated something somewhere but, already four weeks into the programme, I was finding no comfort in the splits. Trying to run laps at an even pace was difficult enough but trying to run two eighty-second laps one after the other was proving beyond me. To make matters worse, looking down at my watch while running was making me lose my form as well as my motivation. It was like having a coach with a clipboard at the side of the track, tutting and shaking his head while noting my times. The very tool I was using to guide my pace was slowing me down. It wasn't until I ignored my watch that I was able to run a little smoother for the last eight hundred metres. Those speed sessions felt like a very different discipline to my long runs and it was clear that I had much to learn about running at that kind of pace.

Even if I lacked skill or experience at the shorter distances, I did have enough determination to keep pushing myself. After dry heaving towards the end of one workout, I jokingly played out the voice of a sadistic coach in my head. He demanded vomit after speed work and for some unknown reason spoke in the broad Texan accent of a cowboy. *You call that a hard session, boy? I don't see no vomit on this here track!* When I ran my next session out of breath but with no sign of potential puking, 'Cowboy Coach' was back. *Where's my vomit, boy?* This was obviously a terrible measure of how well you have run a session, but it did make me consider the effort I was putting into training. Details such as time and pace were useful indicators but the question, *Could I have run better?* covered everything in a few simple words. As I kept my effort consistently high in the three weekly running sessions, my times improved. In just over a month, those 800 metre splits all dropped by ten to fifteen seconds to well under three minutes with quicker recovery times. I was still another ten to fifteen seconds off my target of 2:40 for 800 metres, but my effort was consistently high. Cowboy Coach didn't get to see any vomit but might have grunted some begrudging encouragement. *Not bad, boy, not bad.*

Performance: Practice under pressure

> *"And for your part, won't you come forward and put into practice what you've learned? For it is not fine arguments that are lacking nowadays; no indeed, the books of the Stoics are brimming with them. What is it that is lacking, then? Someone to put them into practice,*

someone to bear witness to the arguments in his actions."
(Epictetus, Discourses, 1.29.55)

Reading a range of sources on when and what to eat, how to warm up, breathe, stretch and stride was useful, but training was the lab where all that theory was put to the test. It's easy to find information, it's much harder to put it into practice. Trialling, adapting and re-testing were the steps that made up an 'experiment of one' to find what worked for me. Unfortunately, knowing what is right doesn't always mean I follow my own hard-earned lessons when I'm under pressure.

That pressure came one evening in the form of mile repeats. They can feel like a much longer race packed into a few minutes. They're long enough to get familiar with the burn in your legs but so intense that you don't feel you have time or space to think. It's just over four laps of a track, but after two you feel as if you have nothing left; yet two more lie ahead. Usually the intensity of speed-work is offset by its brevity, but mile repeats can feel never-ending. I had switched them back from the morning to the evening because they were so challenging. More than any other session, they punished poor preparation or poor running form.

One evening, it only took one mile before I felt as if my stomach was being squeezed and all the oxygen from my lungs pulled out. I could hear Cowboy Coach chuckle beside me, *Gee whiz, boy, you're suffering tonight!* After my second mile, I was doubled over with my straightened arms resting on my knees, the pose of an exhausted runner. I had eaten too close to the session. *Just a little bowl of cereal, a sugar kick before the run,* I'd reasoned. I had previously suffered from eating too close to a speed workout, but I'd gone ahead and ignored the lesson that evening. *I'm in a rush, I'm hungry.* Something so insignificant hurt so much when pressure was applied. Being a little hungry and seeing food was enough to make me discount the wisdom of my own experience. I was trying to improve but was ignoring the little steps to bring me further. That evening at the track reminded me why I need to keep practising the same hard-earned lessons.

Recovery: Stay in tune with mind, body and circumstances

"Virtue may be defined as a habit of mind in harmony with reason and the order of nature." (Cicero, On Invention II.53)

A harmless tweak of a hamstring, that's all it should have been; enough to stop a session but no more. When I pulled up injured during a tempo run, I cut the session short straight away. In the past, I might have struggled on and done more damage, so I was pleased with myself for having the common sense to stop the session. However, I didn't test the extent of the damage either or ask myself any questions about why it had happened. I assumed that a few days of rest would sort it out. I didn't yet have the nous to see it as the warning sign that I should have done. A week later, the warning sign turned into a stop sign.

<u>*Journal Entry: Running to a Stop*</u>
Nine weeks to Cork marathon
Lying on couch, hamstring iced, leg raised

This morning I got up early and had to do an easy two-mile run instead of the speed session as the track was frosty.

I felt that would have set me up well for this evening. I felt good after warming up and started into the mile repeats. The target pace was tough: 5:40 per mile (3:31 per km) pace. I was struggling as I ran six seconds over for the first one and seven for the second. Maybe it was too fast for me, but I was consoling myself that I was still only two to three seconds over the target pace per lap of the crowded track. Slow, slow lap to recover, then I was off again, getting faster, getting better. Two laps later I was gone; hobbling off the track, holding my hamstring. I had done so well to remain relatively injury-free for this training programme, but just at the point when I was beginning to feel my strongest I'm now at my weakest.

Confidence is just arrogance when it's not built on strong foundations. I didn't do a proper warm-down on Sunday. I could have gone for a swim to recover on Monday. I didn't follow a proper warm-up routine either this evening and I still expected top-class results. An inflated ego has brought me crashing back down. I need to ask myself every day, 'Have I done the best I can with the time I have? Will I be disappointed or satisfied with my actions at a later stage?' It seems I still have a lot to learn.

Recovery: Do your best to do things right

"Not to feel exasperated, or defeated, or despondent because your days aren't packed with wise and moral actions. But to get back up when you fail, to celebrate behaving like a human - however imperfectly - and fully embrace the pursuit that you've embarked on." (Marcus Aurelius, Meditations, 5.9)

Whenever I travel, I'm always tempted to take my own path or find a short-cut. However, given my poor sense of direction, my so-called short-cuts usually end up sending me the long way around, backtracking to the starting point. When I discussed my own running programme with people who were training six days a week and completing double my weekly mileage, I thought I had found a way to hack a short-cut to a sub-3-hour marathon. When I started to hit my target paces I thought I must be doing something right, and I was, but I had ignored too many signposts along the way.

I had been noting in my training diary for a few weeks that my left hamstring had been acting up, but I hadn't done anything about it. After the injury, I rested for a few days without any running or cross-training sessions, but I didn't do anything proactive to address the injury either. Just by taking days off, I felt I had done enough to be fit again. Likewise, I wasn't spending as much time as I should have on the work to support my running. I regarded the three running sessions in the programme as being essential, but the two cross-training sessions, warm-up and warm-down routines, core, strength and flexibility sessions were often cut short or left out. Half-measures, while following a low-mileage programme, were increasing my risk of getting, and staying, injured.

Being injured felt like I was stranded at sea, waiting for the wind to pick up so that I could set sail again. Instead of trying to do something proactive, I could only think about how my goal was drifting away. Those thoughts weighed me down and kept me stuck in the doldrums. Little twinges at work would remind me that I couldn't run that evening. Instead of really assessing the injury, I thought more about what I could and should have done prior to that ill-fated session. Getting stuck on the little steps I hadn't taken sent me backwards and I was kicking myself all the way. Without the focus that training gave me, there was a gap that was filled with a cycle of feeling bad, eating worse and doing little.

It took nearly three weeks to get back to running at any sort of decent pace. That little bit of momentum brought my focus back to the present, to what I could do rather than what I couldn't or didn't do. It gave me enough positivity to finally work my way out of that slump. Once I had that perspective, I knew I needed to strengthen my mindset if I wanted to react better in future.

Direction: The less we want to examine our actions, the more likely it is that we need to do it

Journal Entry: Mind the Gap
Six weeks to marathon
Listening to 'River' by Leon Bridges

Long gap since my last journal entry but, having read over some of what I had written, I'm reminded how low I felt just a few weeks ago. I'm so glad to be back running that I'm just focusing on what I can do right now, but I know that I need to react better to injury in future.

On my long run yesterday, I listened to a podcast ('An Irishman Abroad') about a soldier who used writing to help him through some traumatic periods in various conflict zones and later working as a security guard in Haiti ('Broken Ground' by Paddy Doyle). I thought about how writing has helped me in my own, far less challenging, environment yet I hadn't written in my journal for over three weeks. I've thrown myself into working on the house but could easily have found fifteen minutes to review my day. Maybe I didn't want to know. Getting through as much work as I could with as little navel-gazing as possible seemed the best way forward, but I was keeping my head in the sand the whole time.

I had felt so down while injured that I didn't want to look for root causes or long-term solutions. I just wanted quick answers and if I couldn't get them, I wanted distractions. Just when I needed a more positive mindset, I wallowed in self-pity. I'm sure Cowboy Coach would have tutted and hissed, *get your ass off that couch and do something, boy!* It was advice I needed to hear. Instead of feeling sorry for myself, I should have explored the reasons behind my injury. *Why was I injured? Was my training at fault? How could I improve? How could I prevent it from happening again?* When I had most needed the critical voice of writing I'd stopped doing it, and when I got back running, I'd just wanted to charge on without looking back at all the dead-ends and wrong turns I had made. When I wrote in a training diary or journal, it was like having a view from above at the end of each day to look over my tracks to see where they were leading me. Our own mistakes can be our best teachers if we take the time to listen and look. I was only beginning to appreciate this fact, but at least I was trying to pay attention.

CHAPTER 11: RUNNING THE WAY

Self-Awareness: Know, and work, on your strengths and weaknesses

"Thou canst pass thy life in an equable flow of happiness, if thou canst go by the right way, and think and act in the right way." (Marcus Aurelius, Meditations, 5.34)

"Well, what do we have here?" boomed our postgraduate class tutor, Tom. The results page of the personality test covered most of his round face. He appeared to be looking in my direction. Tom's persona was a mix of academic brilliance, eccentricity and devilment. His mind appeared to be perpetually buzzing with new ideas, thoughts and concepts. He had nervous tics that meant he was in perpetual motion: swivelling his head, adjusting his glasses and raising his voice unexpectedly were just a few.

As a class group of professionals in education, we weren't too sure what to make of Tom during our first few tutorials but we all grew to like and admire him. Tom's eccentricity added amusement and bemusement to our late evening classes and made for a jovial atmosphere despite the heavy workload. The module was intended to cover a variety of tools used in personality assessment. Instead of just telling us what kind of tools we could use for personality profiling, Tom arranged for us to take one of the most well-regarded and expensive examples on the market, the '16PF5.'

I noticed the mischievous look that was sparkling behind his square, slightly crooked glasses. "Janey Mac, I haven't seen too many results like yours before!" he commented, his accent heavily rooted in the west of Ireland. He peered over his bifocals to fix his gaze on me. Tom enjoyed the nervous giggles from the rest of the class as the subject of his remarks became apparent. "What have we got here at all, at all? Ha!"

"Well!" he bellowed once again as he placed the results back on the table, his elbows resting on either side as he leaned a little forward. "Let me see here ... *little value in rules and authority and an ability to live in chaos.*" Tom's head twitched to one side and he adjusted his glasses, looking back at me with his hands clasped under his ample chin. He seemed to be trying to figure me out. "We've got a rebel here, ha!" He was discussing one of the factors in the test, perfectionism. He explained how someone with a strong sense of organisation and discipline would score between four and seven. Results at either end of the scale suggested extremes of personality. For example, someone who scored a ten would be very rigid in a work environment and spend far too much time trying to perfect their tasks. The ideal was to be somewhere in the middle of the scale. "This fella here, now! Janey Mac! A score of one, no less!" More giggles erupted around the class. "And would ya lookit' here, no pen nor paper with him either. Ha!"

I sheepishly turned to my perfectionist colleague next to me who dutifully supplied me with one of her many spare pens and some lined paper. "God almighty, a self-control score of two! How did you even make it here this evening?" I joined in the laughter echoing around the room. Tom was now scratching his head, fixing his glasses and rubbing his chin in sequence. "Follows the wind, this fella." Then, he leaned way back in his chair with his arms folded and when Tom spoke next, his voice was more serious. "But don't be laughing too hard at him! High scores in reasoning and abstractedness as well; this man can see the bigger picture when he wants to." Tom was still and quiet for just a second. "If he can get his head out of the feckin' clouds!"

I had to agree with most of the results. Despite what you have read so far, my natural disposition is opposed to set structures, being told what to do, and environments that are too rigid. If I'm ordered to go one way, I'll head off in the opposite direction. It often means I get lost for a while, but I prefer to make it there in my own way. Backpacking in a variety of faraway destinations has indulged my innate independence but has also highlighted my stumbling and bumbling ways. It has led to delays, detours and mishaps aplenty: missed flights, lost passports, illegal entry into Honduras, waking up on a bus having travelled five hours in the wrong direction in Colombia, and detention by immigration officers after a long night in Tijuana, Mexico, to name a few.

Running gave me the structure that I needed and wanted. Changing sports and long periods of travel had covered up a lack of progress but running always told me exactly where I was. The challenge of the marathon meant I had to work on my weaknesses: practicalities and consistent preparation. It's easy to sign up for a marathon these days, but I wanted to do it right. Shorter races had let me get away with less than ideal training but preparing for my first marathon meant building blocks of training, month after month. Developing and following a daily routine gave me a better chance of fitting in all the elements that marathon training involves. Even the smallest changes had significant benefits over time. Preparing my training gear, the night before an early run meant it was harder to come up with excuses the next day. Having set routines to follow for warming up and down, nutrition and stretching meant fewer decisions to make and less chance of me skipping them. Routine gave me mental energy to focus on what was more important: focussing on running well rather than getting ready. For a guy who hated systems and rules, they were providing the scaffolding for me to start reaching my potential.

Nutrition was another area where I was slowly improving and maintaining some consistency. On one of my first long runs, my only sustenance was a few Minstrels (chocolate sweets) grabbed while rushing out the door but by the time I was towards the end of the training programme, my diet was cleaned up to include a lot more vegetables, meat, beans, nuts, lentils and fish. I tried to drink around two litres of water a day, but often replaced some of this with cups of herbal tea. One sacrifice I had considered was cutting out coffee but, like the pre-election promises of an eager politician, it was never going to happen. I compromised by keeping it down to two sittings of coffee a day, which probably meant three to four cups. It can appear rigid when it's all written down, but I found that to be freeing rather than fettering. It cleared the way for me to focus on the greater challenges that lay ahead.

Nutrition: Learn from your mistakes

> *"First of all, condemn what you are doing, and then when you have condemned it, do not despair of yourself, and be not in the condition of those men of mean spirit, who, when they have once given in, surrender themselves completely and are carried away as if by a torrent. But see what the trainers of boys do. Has the boy fallen? Rise, they say, wrestle again till you are made strong ... for from within comes ruin and from within comes help."*
> (Epictetus, Discourses, 4.9)

I would love to say that once I had a settled structure and routine I always followed it, but that was not the case. My diet had been relatively nutritious and healthy throughout my marathon training, with a cheat-day every week to indulge in whatever I wanted. However, when I went on a working trip to Copenhagen cheat-day became cheat-week. After wandering around the damp, Danish streets on arrival looking for the hotel, I warmed myself by taking full advantage of the complimentary coffee and pastries in the lobby for the duration of a soccer match. Abandoning all dietary common sense left me with a sugar and caffeine hangover later, but I reasoned that it was better than going out drinking beer for the afternoon as I would have done in the past.

The rest of the week followed much the same pattern. Our morning and afternoon snacks were wheeled out between presentations: large carafes of coffee and glistening pastries. I indulged heavily in both. It wasn't all sugar-coated deliciousness, as our main meals were all healthy with plenty of wholesome rye bread, but by the end of the week I literally could not move. A week of bread and pastries had brought me and my digestion to a standstill. An early-morning jog had to be cut short after a few minutes because it felt as if I were carrying around a large stone in my stomach. I felt blocked and ready to burst at the same time. I was denied my run around one of the city's beautiful lakes and had to waddle back to the hotel instead. My stomach stayed like that for a few more days, flaring up if I went near anything containing wheat. I thought of Tom and his personality test; I still needed to break the rules and mess up every so often to remind myself why they were there in the first place.

PART V: RUNNING AND LEARNING

CHAPTER 12: RUNNING FREE

Recovery: Never let go easily

"Persist and resist." (Epictetus, Discourses, 10)

Three weeks to the marathon and I ran one of my final speed sessions before tapering. It should have filled me with confidence, but the disappointing splits flooded my mind and washed away any enthusiasm. My hands were clasped over my bowed head as I walked to recover. My senses sought distraction in the warm May breeze, the sound of the cars whirring by, the setting sun. They were all more welcome than the reality of my sub-3-hour hopes slipping away.

I felt ready and able to run the marathon distance but suspected that my hamstring hadn't healed enough to run it at a sub-3-hour pace (6:50 mile/ 4:15 km). I felt like a workhorse wanting to escape with a gallop but, like reins, that hamstring was pulling me back to a canter. The last full speed session just before the taper was five by 1 km repeats at 5:22 mile pace (3:20 km). I tried hard, but I ran them more like a tempo run with 6:00 miles (3:44 km). I had chosen to run on a section of the marathon course that would be around mile twenty-two. It is locally referred to as 'the straight road' and inevitably has a headwind in whatever direction you are running. I couldn't see how I could maintain a sub-3-hour pace and then face into a headwind after 22 miles. My state of fitness didn't bode well for running a marathon, even less so for a sub-3-hour marathon. But runners don't let go easily. Hard miles train you to deal with pain and doubt and I was going to have to face a lot more of both.

Pain was served in the form of therapy and the torture was dished out by the steel hands of Mike. In my experience of physiotherapy, the chattier the therapist, the more pain they seem to inflict. Mike was no different. Digging deep into scar tissue, he started casually chatting about the weather, the Cork football team and eventually my training. "Hasn't been going that well lately," I managed to reply as I gripped the side of the massage table. "Paces way off," my voice wavered as he dug deeper. "Haven't run at a decent speed for a while." Mike carried on happily chatting as he moved on to relieve the tension in my lower back by pushing down on my pelvis. "My goal time? Ah. I had been hoping for a sub-3-hour". Silence, apart from the bones cracking in my back.

I said no more. I was lying on my back, my right knee on my left hip with a man putting most of his weight on my pelvis; a position that doesn't lend itself to chit-chat. My last words were still echoing inside my head. It made me reflect on what I had said: time out due to injury, missed training, slower paces. My target suddenly seemed more of a hope than an aim. Mike made it very clear that I should be cautious with my pacing, as I still lacked flexibility in my hamstring and it was my first marathon. I knew he was trying to dance around saying, "No chance", but what he actually said was, "Take it easy. No one races their first." A smack on my leg sounded the end of the session. Reality was making itself clear in different ways, but I still had two weeks left and was going to delay coming to any conclusions. I tried to squeeze in as much stretching, strength work and faster paces as I could during that time without pushing myself too much.

The night before the marathon, it was time to face reality and come up with a race plan. At that time, I used to run races with a cheap digital watch and a paper wristband with target splits on it to guide my pacing, so printing out a pace-band was the final fitness test. Agitated and unsure, I was sitting in front of a computer screen that flickered in a dark room. Fidgeting with the keyboard, right foot tapping the ground under the table, delaying the inevitable. It made sense to follow Mike's advice and just focus on completing the marathon. "No one races their first". But the mind of a runner isn't very good at listening: it wants to run more, longer, or faster. Hopes of a sub-3-hour time still hung in the air and I was clinging on to every one of them. *I've done some marathon-paced miles at the end of long runs. I could probably keep up a 6:50 mile (4:15 km) pace for twenty miles (32 km).* I ignored the fact that I had never run longer than twenty miles and that doing it for the first time tired and injured probably wasn't a great idea.

Looking back at my training diary, I could see there were quite a few gaps. I had followed a low-mileage programme, but injury had cut it down even more. *But is it not worth a gamble?* Time for bed and time to decide. I clicked the 'print' button and there it was: reality made clear in black and white. My mile paces were set at 7:10 with a target time of 3 hours 9 minutes. I surprised myself with a sigh of relief. The time was set, and my gear was ready. Satisfied with my decision, I sealed the pace-band with clear tape and yet still, I could still hear the runner's voice in the back of my mind. *I'll keep the sub-3-hour group within sight for a while. Maybe there's still a chance.*

Race Report: Cork City Marathon

Anticipation bubbled beneath the surface, the air brimmed with energy despite runners doing their best to conserve it. Music blared as we lined up where it all would begin and end, St. Patrick's Street. There was a coolness in the air, but the skies promised sunshine. Everyone had their own way of spending those last few minutes before we set off: some smiled, some stared, some jumped on the spot, others were fixed to it. My mind was strangely calm and relaxed. I hadn't been too sure how I would feel after weeks of doubt about my hamstring but as soon as I saw the starting line, all those anxious thoughts and concerns faded away. The challenge was there waiting, regardless of whether I was ready or not. The time had come, and the race was going to start with or without me. At that point, there was nothing more I could do to prepare. My mental and physical training would have to take it the rest of the way.

For the few minutes before the start of the race I just felt light, excited to begin. I even started to smile but instinctively cupped my hands over my mouth, faking a yawn and told myself to put on more of a 'game' face. I should have enjoyed that moment more. It's rare that a smile like that comes from deep in the belly through your chest to spread across your face without being conscious of it until it's too powerful to ignore. On that sunny morning, standing at the starting line of a marathon, smiling like a loon, I felt as if I were beginning something more important than a mere race. A countdown began. People shuffled forward even further. The starting gun was fired, and we were off.

For that first mile, it felt as if I were looking down at myself from above. *Am I really doing this? Am I about to run a marathon through the streets of Cork?* I think I was still trying to reconcile myself to the reality of starting such a long journey. No matter how much I prepare for something important, I will inevitably suffer a little jolt of doubt just before I take the first step. The greatest reassurance in the world is to be able to respond with absolute clarity, *this is where I want to be and what I want to do*. As we crossed over the river Lee on the third mile, I repeated those words with absolute certainty.

I soon fell into stride with a runner who had vocal supporters dotted along the course urging him on. I basked vicariously in the applause directed towards him, until the crowds eventually dwindled. We didn't speak but it felt good to run alongside someone with a similar stride, feeling stronger as we stepped along in sync. Even though I had decided on a sub-3:10 marathon, I still harboured ambitions of conjuring up a sub-3-hour time, *there might still be a chance*. We could still see the balloon of the 3-hour pace group in the distance. When the runner alongside me eventually asked me what time I was hoping for, I replied, "Sub-3:10, but I want to keep an eye on the sub-3-hour group." Hearing it out loud made me realise how foolish it sounded. Runner's belligerence had blinded me to the obvious: no one eases into a pace over twenty-five seconds faster per mile than planned (ten seconds per kilometre) in a marathon. Following that balloon mindlessly would have been chasing disaster. Those missed weeks of training weren't coming back. I had to accept where I was, rather than where I wanted to be.

It still wasn't going to be easy to run six miles further than I had ever done before and at a decent pace, 7:15 per mile (4:25 per km). I was beginning to overthink the run. Inhaling deeply for three seconds, exhaling harder for two seconds, I mentally scanned my body to filter out any loss of form. Simple reminders kept me running one step at a time: *run tall, core strong, hands loose.*

The same runner stayed next to me and we ran shoulder to shoulder for another few miles. It can feel like a solid connection when someone is toiling beside you with a shared aim, whether words are spoken or not. He looked more like a hardened footballer than a runner but was moving smoothly. When he offered me a drink of water from a water-station bottle I guessed from his accent that he was a Kerryman. I didn't take up his offer of water as I wanted to avoid the prospect of a toilet stop later. When I had stopped on previous occasions, I had found it difficult to get my legs going again afterwards. The big Kerryman glugged back another mouthful, pausing for a moment before casually advising me out of the side of his mouth, "Yerra, if you need the toilet just piss away in the shorts." He reasoned that no one would take any notice of my shorts, given all the water that ends up on them anyway. I knew cyclists did this but had never heard of a runner advising it. I didn't think he was serious and thought it was another case of a Kerryman very literally trying to take the piss out of a Corkman. Although I didn't take his advice, I stopped worrying about the need to stop; in the worst-case scenario, I could consider that undesirable course of action. Contemplating the worst-case scenario freed my mind from worry and I took some of the Kerryman's water. In the end, I didn't even relieve myself until well after the race – in a toilet.

The Kerryman had disclosed earlier that we were chasing the same race goal and had grunted that we should stick together but "No talking!" However, once we had clocked up some miles together, the mutterings and little exchanges grew to a conversation. As with most people from the 'kingdom', we ended up talking about football. The chat could have taken place on a high stool in any pub as we discussed our counties' prospects for the season ahead. Talking let the time go by a little easier as we passed mile 10. "Too feckin' easy!" the Kerryman exclaimed after checking his GPS watch. Our pace had matched our conversation as we'd lost about forty seconds on that mile alone. "No talking!" was once again the rule.

Running Tip: Running Form

Everyone has a lazy runner in them: the posture we assume when our running muscles get tired and want other body parts to do some extra work. My lazy runner runs in an 'ass back, head forward, eyes down' pose. The quickest way to get rid of the lazy runner is to imagine Cowboy Coach pulling me up by both ears. *I told you to run tall, boy!* There are so many ways for people to run and you can see them all in a marathon: racing and shuffling, gliding and grinding, heel striking and toe-tipping, head-wobbling and tongue-wagging. The experiment you conduct on yourself through training should lead you to the style that best suits you.

We picked up the pace for the next mile in silence. I tried to stay conscious of my stride to ensure that I wasn't pushing my body too hard. Easy breathing and strong form were telling me I was at the right pitch. I had to keep reminding myself to keep it that way. Running too fast would tire out my legs or lungs and make me lose my form. That's when my lazy running style would kick in. If I can't keep my form, I know I need to slow down.

Running Tip: Secret technique

Another little technique I like to use when racing is one that I have rarely seen or heard mentioned by anyone else. Don't get your hopes up and think it's some sort of magic: it's simply smiling during a race. Maybe there's a bit of hippy in me, but it really adds to my running if I can smile, high-five or wave at supporters. The logical side of me believes it's effective because it relaxes my face, which in turn loosens my neck, shoulders and back. The hippy and logician in me both know that if I can smile when under pressure, I've already arrived somewhere even before reaching the finish.

Cork City Marathon Part II: Halfway to Paradise

The Kerryman, however, was not smiling nearing the halfway point. I felt our pace drop a little after passing mile 12 but had kept my mouth shut. He had earlier outlined his own race strategy, "Keep the pace even, no going mad." In a rare lapse into open conversation, he had disclosed how he'd made several attempts to break 3 hours 10 minutes for the marathon. As he spoke, his gruff demeanour had softened, and his words were almost wistful as if that target loomed overhead, agonisingly just out of reach.

Coming up with a pacing strategy for a marathon is not easy. It's like trying to drive somewhere as fast as you can with just enough fuel to get you there. Go too fast, too soon and you can end up running on fumes at the end, stuttering to the finish line. Going slower will give you a far better chance of finishing strong, but if you don't empty the tank you're left with fuel for regret. The challenge with running is that you can't gauge your energy source. Sticking to some sort of pre-race plan can help eliminate some of the guesswork, but at times you need to react to whatever is unfolding in front of you. Passing the halfway point in this race was one of those times.

My watch read 1:33:45. We were on pace with about two minutes to spare. The first half had been on mostly flat terrain but there were a lot of harder miles ahead. My gut said they would cost us more than two minutes. Picking up the pace to 'bank' time for later could have burned my legs, but I knew that if I didn't I would struggle to make time on the harder miles ahead and break 3:10. There were still some easier miles left as we looped around the path on Jacob's Island, which was flat as a pancake. Someone had spray-painted *Halfway to Paradise* on the ground beneath our feet, but I felt sure I would have to pass through hell first. It was time to react.

We had merged with a pack of runners and had gradually slowed down to match their pace. I edged my way through the group, looking back to beckon the Kerryman to follow my lead. He was in the middle of the pack when I tried to catch his eye, but his head was down. The next time I glanced back, I expected to see him following just behind me; instead, I was further ahead of the group and he was nowhere to be seen. The course switched from a wide expanse of marine views to a narrow section following an old railway line. There were trees to either side of me on a steep embankment and very few supporters. I glanced to the side out of habit, expecting the grunting Kerryman to be there. I only missed the company when it was gone. I had run this route many times on my own, but right then I felt alone; just me, with many miles to go.

I indulged in my own little pity party for a few moments before snapping out of it to refocus on the distance ahead. The Kerryman was an experienced runner and knew what was best for him. Either of us compromising for the other one would have been counter-productive; we each had our own race to run. It was at times like this that my old hurling mentor, Con, would hitch up his pants, wave his fists in front of him and declare it was time to "Die dog or eat the hatchet." As a teenager I never fully understood the phrase, but I think he meant we always have a choice to either roll over or face up to the pain of a challenge. I was about to find out what kind of appetite I had.

Reaching fifteen miles, I had about three minutes to spare in the time-bank for the harder miles ahead. I was already beginning to feel the fatigue in my legs so the ensuing inclines and rolling hills, however small, took their toll. I knew I was losing a little time, but I was giving my all. Times and paces became less important as reaching the crest of the next hill became my only focus. Doubts were creeping back in after running seventeen miles; another nine seemed like an eternity. I tried to take strength from my surroundings. My first name was printed on my race-bib and supporters called it out. It helped but all I could give in return was a thumbs-up and a weak smile. Then a familiar voice shouted out my surname with some encouragement. That was all I needed: simple words at the right time. It snapped me out of my reverie and lifted me enough to run tall again.

Cork City Marathon Part III: Running into the Unknown

As I passed the 20-mile mark (32-km), I was still running on my own between groups. The physical stress was building up, but I felt a thrilling gulp of fear as I ran into unknown territory. *Would the missed weeks of training come back to haunt me? Would my hamstring give up on me?* The answers were on the way, whether I wanted them or not. I had deliberately finished my last long run on the same rolling hills of Model Farm Road to help prepare myself mentally for the pain. I pre-empted emotions that would try to deceive my eyes into imagining the hills were far bigger than I knew them to be. I kept my thoughts simple: *run what you can see, keep your shape.*

A group of musicians played samba drums and happy tunes. My thumbs were up but my smile was more like a grimace. My left hamstring began to creak and complain but I tried not to listen. It was just another voice of complaint among many. I only thought of getting to the next mile on the 'straight road'. Grabbing a sports drink, I took a few small sips. I was breaking the running rule of never doing something in a race that you haven't done in training, but I had never run twenty-two miles either. I had trained on this part of the course many times, visualising myself running strong even though I knew I would be exhausted. At mile 23, I clung desperately to that image.

The groaning pain from my hamstring prodded and poked at my thin veneer of strength. I felt as if I were running on thin ice, each step creating little cracks that threatened to bring me down. Sporadic cheers from supporters weren't enough anymore; I was running in my own little bubble of pain and fatigue.

My thoughts narrowed to survival mode. *Run what you can see, run what you can see.* The problem with running on the straightest road in Cork is that you can see quite far. I was getting pissed off at this point, annoyed that there was still so much left to go. You've come such a long way, but you have another three miles to run into the unknown, on top of the last three. *This is stupid, this is madness. Surely twenty-three miles is enough to deserve a medal!* I was glad to leave the 'straight road' and join the more sheltered, leafy environs of the Mardyke, that are featured in song. Despite the claims of the lyrics, my heart was not as light *as the wild winds that blow through each elm tree.* I was feeling the weight of the miles and my head and shoulders were dropping. As I looped closer to bridging the river Lee again, someone crossed right in front of me, shouting something. My addled brain couldn't decipher his words until I was past him. "Great running. This is what you trained for!" His words stuck with me. *This is what I trained for.* It was time to eat that hatchet.

The course took us over a foot-bridge on to a narrow path with trees on either side. My world darkened as if I was running through a narrow tunnel with the walls closing in. I peered straight ahead, ignoring the darkness surrounding me. Passing some older half-marathon runners, they urged me on "G'wan boy, fair play!" I was running tall again. Then there was a sudden burst of light as the course spilled out on to North Mall. A little further and then I could see it, the last bridge, St. Patrick's Bridge. It arched and shone like it never had before; the end lay just half a mile away. I still remember it as one of the most intensely fulfilling times of my life. Waves of emotion elevated my mind and body and lifted my legs for one last effort. I took the last incline leading up to the bridge and picked up the tempo to what felt like a 10-km pace. If my hamstring went, I was close enough to hobble to the finish. Thumping music beckoned us home. I looked skyward and thought of my brother. A well of emotion was on the verge of overflowing, but it wasn't the time for thoughts or tears; it was time to let go. There were no runners around me so even though the crowd was cheering everyone home, it was easy to feel that their appreciation was all for me. I returned the applause before raising my arms to the side with opened hands. In those few moments running fast and free down the middle of Cork city, I felt more powerful than I could ever have imagined. I crossed the line empty and exhausted but full of emotion. Loved ones waiting at the end made the experience even more special with hugs, kisses and smiles all round. The feeling in those moments went a long way to answering the question I started with: Why do I run?

Attitude: Celebrate effort, not the passing of time

"Count your years, and you will be ashamed to desire and pursue the same things you desired in your boyhood days." (Seneca, Letters from a Stoic, 27. 2)

My finishing time? It's one of the few parts of the day that is not an emotive memory for me. Little moments were relished and are still treasured with a glow that digits on a screen can never match: lunch in the sun with Angie, Mum and Dad and the first sup of creamy Beamish stout with my heavy legs swinging loose from a high stool. Food and pints earned by effort always taste better. Pushing my limits reminds me to appreciate the simple things and reminds me of what is important. Finishing in 3:08 was just the icing on the cake. I might have done better if I hadn't missed weeks of training, but I refused to dwell on hypothetical times. In the end, I got what I deserved.

I'm not too sure if I deserved a hotel break, but Angie and I checked into a seaside hotel in Kinsale the next day for some relaxation and recovery. She had been a great support throughout my training, enduring my high, lows and early morning starts, and she deserved some pampering. I was probably looking forward to the princess treatment more than she was, but we both enjoyed lounging by the pool all day before dinner and drinks. It might seem like excessive basking in the glory of what was essentially a long run, but I think it's important to mark and reward achievements. Celebrating milestones such as birthdays never has much meaning for me. To acclaim one such day over another is to value the passing of time; nothing changes except that you are one day older. Celebrating your efforts instead reminds you that 'making your mark' on time is of more value than marking your time.

Over the next few days, I inevitably started to think about what to do next. I tried to let these thoughts come and go, knowing they would return. It can be tempting to keep looking forward to the next goal, but it's only by looking back that you realise how far you've come. Moving on too quickly would have belittled the efforts of the previous months so I've included a summary of practical running tips and cues that worked for me at the end of Book I.

Consistency: The Next Step

For two weeks, I enjoyed the ease of not having to focus on anything. It was like drifting downriver in a boat on a sunny day, moving just enough to neither need nor want to pick up the oars. I was on holidays from work, so my routine was open and flexible. I meandered along, filling up my time without really going anywhere. I knew I wouldn't remember anything I was doing two months later or even a few weeks on, so I decided to sit down to plan my goals and give some direction to the months ahead. Those goals covered different areas of my life, but the prospect of running another marathon in less than three hours never strayed too far from my mind. *'Run the Dublin City Marathon under 3 hours'.* Words written on a page never fail to give a sense of purpose and place to thoughts that once floated without direction or destination. Once I had set that sub-3-hour target for Dublin, I thought about how I should get there.

After doing some research on marathon plans, I decided to stick with the FIRST programme. The intensity of the sessions and low mileage suited me and, more importantly, I felt it was something I could incorporate with the rest of my life. Training for this marathon was going to be much easier as I had already put my body through one marathon cycle, knew a lot more about nutrition, paces and routine and had four full months to get ready. Unfortunately, I still didn't have enough experience to keep in mind that training rarely goes to plan. It transpired that it was two months before I completed a full week of training. Just when I thought the path was clear, I had to find a different way.

Lessons from Cork marathon

These are reminders of what I've learned through training. They were written for me, but you may find them useful.

Focus
- Remember the things you cannot control; be brave in changing the things you can; be wise enough to know the difference.
- Find your challenge: It should be intimidating yet exciting.
- Do the work, today: You can only shape the future in the present.
- Keep your eyes open but only focus on what is important.
- When the going gets heavy, just hang on: It's not always going to be easy or pretty. Hanging on is sometimes as good as it gets.
- Failure in the present shouldn't detract from your future: The pain of failure is natural, but you must learn to move on when your feelings affect your future and the people around you.
- Set your own high standards: Be your own boss.

Routine
- Use routine to channel your energy to what really matters.
- Be persistent and consistent: It beats intensity in the long term.
- Eat as well as you can as often as you can: Eat junk food if you need it to remind you why you try to eat well.
- Use or love the things you own: Otherwise your possessions just get in the way.

Tracking
- Keep your balance: Your successes shouldn't send your spirits too high nor should you let your failures send you too low.
- Turn mistakes into lessons by learning from them.
- Channel your thoughts: If you're thinking too much, they need to go somewhere. Talk, write, run - do whatever suits you.
- Take stock every day: Observe any warning signs and ask what they are telling you. The days you don't want to take stock are the times that you need to most.

Running Tips
When I scan my body for running form, these are the cues and form checks that I make.

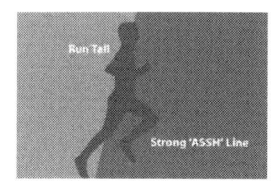

- Run Tall: Head up, eyes up, body straight. Imagine a string lifting you up from the top of head. If all else fails, try to keep running tall.
- Shoulders Back, Shoulders Down: Shoulders relaxed. If they tense up, drop arms, shake them out and reset shoulders back and down into a relaxed position.
- Loose Pistol Hands: Hands loose and relaxed with thumbs on fist. Swing them up along the body just far enough to see from the corner of your eye and then back to your hips, like drawing a pistol.

- Propeller Arms: Arms straight, powering you forward.
- Steel Barrel: Imagine the middle of your body as a steel barrel that supports everything above and below and is upright enough to carry water. Pull your navel towards your spine to keep the core under a little tension. Keep your lower back flat.
- Belly Breathe, Chest Out, Exhale Hard: Inhale by lifting bottom of belly towards spine and filling chest with air.
- Enjoy it all: Smile and give high-fives and thumbs-up whenever you can.

RUNNING FOR BETTER - BOOK II: CORK TO DUBLIN CITY MARATHON

CHAPTER 13 – BACK TO THAILAND

Consistency: Expect that life will not always go to plan
Replay Residence, Bang-Rak Beach, Koh Samui, July 2014

"What are you aiming at? What's your goal? All that's to come, lies in uncertainty: live right now." (Seneca, On the Shortness of Life, 9.1)

    The breeze from the gym air-con was instantly refreshing. The morning heat had already felt intense during the short walk across the apartment complex. I hopped on the only treadmill in the gym and started a slow jog. My towel was hanging to my left side and there was a water bottle on my right. A TV screen was fixed in front of me and dance music blared around the gym. Later, I could tick off the completed tempo session in the app. version of the FIRST programme. Everything was set.

    After five minutes, I gradually increased the treadmill pace towards my target time. My legs felt heavy and my left hamstring tight, but after ten minutes or so I slowly increased the pace. I felt in control and ready to push on. I was thinking, *this training cycle is going to be as straightforward as marathon training gets.* The treadmill took that thought as a cue to jam suddenly, almost sending me flying out the back of it. I grabbed the side rails, but not before the knee of my standing leg had locked and jarred. I thought the worst as I stepped off and sat down holding my leg as if it were about to fall off. I had enough issues with muscle and tendon injuries without adding knees to my list of woes. After some heavy breathing, leg extensions and a few grimaces, I concluded that it would be okay but that the gym wasn't going to get me into marathon shape or even maintain my fitness. It had seemed my best option for running, as the Thai roads were either very busy or had uneven surfaces. I could have awoken early to avoid the traffic and the worst of the heat, but I still wouldn't have managed any quality sessions. I could now see that, with all the willpower in the world, the 'perfect plan' wasn't going to work.

It was time to reassess. Instead of considering what I should do next, I looked at what I could do next and what my environment had to offer. I wanted something physically demanding that would benefit my marathon training, but I didn't want to spend mind-numbing hours on elliptical machines or exercise bikes in the gym. I had stayed fit from boxing the previous year but there were no 'western boxing' gyms nearby. The obvious option, given my environment, was Muay Thai boxing. I rapidly came up with a list of reasons against doing it: I had never done it before, my hip flexibility was terrible, and there was a risk of injury from the amount of kicking involved. The alternative was aqua-jogging and the exercise bikes in the gym; I signed up to a Muay Thai gym the next day.

CHAPTER 14: BACK TO BOXING

Mindset: Stay steady until you get stronger

> *"Fortune has often in the past got the upper hand of you, and yet you have not surrendered, but have leaped up and stood your ground still more eagerly. For manliness gains much strength by being challenged."*
> *(Seneca, Letters from a Stoic, 13.2)*

English words spoken in a Thai accent bellowed throughout the gym: "Shadow Box! Five minute." Even I can do this part, I thought. In front of a wall of mirrors, about fifteen of us were puffing, shuffling and trying out boxing combinations. Alongside us a row of trainers was keenly observing the movements of the students. I soon noticed that my stance and punching style were different to everyone else's; mine was a narrow, evasive, western boxing stance and theirs a wide, frontal, Thai boxing stance. I tried to adjust my footing but found it difficult to do so while shadow-boxing at the same time. One of the trainers demonstrated how I should stand; I quietly nodded and tried to replicate the position as best I could. After a minute or so, however, I slipped back into my old stance. A different trainer, Noi, came over to demonstrate the same change in stance, to which I responded, "Yeah, I know. I keep thinking I'm boxing." Unfortunately for me, the only words he understood were "I know". His face hardened for a moment while his eyes betrayed the anger that flickered within him. Showing respect to your teacher is very important in Thai culture, and he thought I was dismissing his advice. He would make himself heard in many ways over the next two weeks.

Muay Thai wasn't going to be as mentally taxing as boxing for me, as I was at too low a level to work on combinations, but the 'art of eight limbs' is the most brutal fighting form I know. In boxing you're restricted to fighting with your hands, but Muay Thai boxers strike with the fists, elbows, knees and shins. Every blow is designed to inflict as much damage as possible. The circuit training followed the same pattern of physical attrition. Training started slowly in the cooler early morning air with a twenty-minute jog but became more intense as the sun got hotter. It started with hundreds of repetitions of upper body exercises and core-work. A quick water-break before relentless repetitions of punching and kicking drills: punches, elbows, low kicks, high-knees, high kicks all into heavy bags. My technique became sloppy as sweat began to pour and breath was hard to catch. A water break, more conditioning exercises, then pad-work with other fighters and pad-work in the ring with one of the trainers. The last ten minutes were filled with more core and bodyweight exercises. Trainers watched to see if we were doing them properly and made us do them again if we skipped any repetitions. They ensured that we emptied every remaining joule of energy before ending a brutally tough two-hour workout.

Our training still paled in comparison to what some western fighters were doing in the training camp. There were two brothers from Georgia (formerly part of the Soviet Union) who trained separately from us. Small of stature, every part of their bodies was muscle, sinew and bone. Nothing was wasted, including their time. They lived, slept and ate in the training camp spending their days working on sparring, technique and conditioning. They finished their first session of the day by raising and lowering a concrete block hanging from their heads to strengthen their neck muscles. I could barely lift my bottle of water by that point.

Muay Thai wasn't the best training for a marathon, but it felt great to have done such a tough workout by 10:00 a.m., knowing you had already accomplished a lot that day. As the week went by, the routine became more familiar: rise at 7:10, check scores from the World Cup in Brazil, drink water, eat a small banana, get ready and hop on the scooter for a twenty-minute ride in rush-hour traffic. It felt surreal at times to wait at red lights wiping sleep from my eyes with the chaos of Thai traffic buzzing all around me.

One of the last parts of the session was pad-work and we would be called upon to work with different trainers when we weren't paired with other fighters. Noi always chose me, beckoning me up to the ring with a tilt of his head. He even had his own nickname for me, 'I know', which I would overhear him say to the other trainers. Noi was very different to most Thais in his appearance and behaviour; he had long, straight, jet-black hair and dark leathery skin which covered his stout frame. He reminded me of a stereotypically gruff Native American elder. Thais can be very kind and light-hearted, but Noi's dour demeanour made him an exception.

The pad-work was intended to practise the combinations we had learned earlier in the session, but Noi had his own interpretation; whenever my kicks were too slow, he would sweep my standing leg and send me crashing to the mat. I was getting payback for a perceived slight. Any mistakes I made in the basic combinations, of which there were many, were punished with press-ups. I listened to the few words he said, kept my mouth shut and stuck with it. My kicks were slow to improve but I pounded out those punishment press-ups as if I were in training for the army. Whenever he told me to drop and do twenty, I snapped my way through them before popping back up. I was on the verge of vomiting a few times but tried not to let it show. Stand your ground, I repeated to myself even though in this instance, it meant being on it for much of the time.

Admittedly, I wasn't jumping out of bed for training every morning as easier options floated to mind: *skip it today, you're on holidays, you don't have to do this.* It would have been easy to turn over for a lie-in, but Noi inspired me to keep going; I didn't want to give him the satisfaction of me skipping a session. I had made my plan, paid my money and I intended to stick it out. Long-term gains invariably require short-term pain. After two bruising weeks, I was glad to finish but satisfied that I had persisted with the training. At the end of every session, we gave thanks to each of the trainers, who lined up in a row at the top of the gym, with the traditional Thai greeting, 'Wai' – our hands clasped as if in prayer and brought to our bowed foreheads. On my last day, part of me was hoping for a begrudging grunt of approval from Noi. Unsurprisingly it never came, but I was ready to move on.

CHAPTER 15: FINDING AIR

Attitude: Look for solutions, not excuses

> *"Very little is needed to make a happy life; it is all within yourself, in your way of thinking." (Marcus Aurelius, Meditations, 7.67)*

After two weeks of Muay Thai training in the morning and swimming at least a mile every afternoon, I was feeling fit, but I needed to run some miles back into my legs. Scouting the island on afternoon scooter rides, I found a way to run safely while still enjoying our holiday. There was an open-air gym on the other side of the island, on the top floor of a building covered by a roof but open at the sides. From that height, the sea views were inspiring and the sea air refreshing.

We decided to join the gym for a week and took a room at a hotel across the road with a small pool. The hotel was basic but had lots of 'character', which meant it had rustic charm or was run-down, depending on your preferred level of comfort. The eccentric owner was more concerned with the welfare of her cats than her guests, but we loved relaxing by the pool, enjoying the great views and being so close to the gym.

The next morning, I got up early to avoid the heat as much as possible. I started slowly on the treadmill and felt fresh for the first thirty minutes, as the sea air did its best to keep me cool. As I picked up the pace, however, it grew much more difficult and sweat poured down my face. I wasn't even going fast, covering just over five miles (8.5 km) in forty minutes. In Ireland, I sweated only when running at a very high intensity; in Thailand, my body was overheating before my legs had a chance to warm up. I was beginning to feel that no matter what I did, it wasn't enough. Although I had set up everything to make running as easy as possible, I was still struggling to make progress.

That afternoon, we went for a scooter ride towards the west of the island which cooled us down as we whirred along sea roads and up hilly paths to green forest. The beautiful views and streams of air refreshed us once again, and I began to see things more clearly. Whatever my misgivings about my training, I had to remember that I was fit and able to train every day, had enough money to eat and sleep well and had someone I loved by my side. To top it all off, I was doing this on a beautiful island off the coast of Thailand. It was time to appreciate the charmed life I was living and to be grateful for whatever training I could do. Everything I needed and wanted was right there in front of me. So, what if I couldn't run for longer than an hour and had to run twice a day to get in more mileage? At least I was running. I would do my best and be happy with that. When we got back to the hotel that evening, we went for a refreshing dip in the pool and watched the sun set across the island. It wasn't difficult to feel grateful, but more than anything I felt calmer. *Just do all you can* was my mantra for that week. As mosquitoes began to buzz overhead, I grabbed my gear and headed to the gym for another session.

By the end of the week I had managed around

forty miles (64 km) that included one long run of ninety minutes and a few marathon-paced miles. It wasn't going to have me running a fast marathon, but it was all I could do. The week's training had been enjoyable, interspersed with lazy afternoon coffees, great Thai food, a couple of beers on most days and scooter rides around the island every day. We loved the mix of a daily routine juxtaposed with the exotic sights and smells that surrounded us or as Thais would say, 'same, same but different'. But almost as soon as our routine had settled we were off to our next stop, Ho Chi Minh city in Vietnam.

CHAPTER 16: FINDING ANSWERS IN VIETNAM

Gratitude: Remember that being free enough to run is to be rich

> *"It is not the man who has too little, but the man who craves more, that is poor."* (Seneca, Letters from a Stoic, 2.6)

The enveloping noise, motion and commotion of Vietnamese cities were familiar to me, but it was Angie's first time in Vietnam. Ho Chi Minh city combined all her Asian experiences up to that point and amplified them in a city packed with eight million people, all of them in a hurry. We enjoyed the unique charm of the city but not the mix of perspiration and pollution we experienced while walking around it. On our first morning, we walked to a local park to go for an easy jog; however, after ten minutes of draining heat, cracked pavement and limited space I gave up, something I very rarely do. We decided to move after a short stay but instead of meandering own way up the country with short journeys we decided we would find somewhere we really liked and spend more time there.

The place we chose was a little town called Hoi-An. After a few days, it became clear that Hoi-An encapsulated everything we wanted from a travel destination – family-run accommodation with free bikes, glasses of beer at ten cents each, a nearby beach, space to run and, to top it all off, lots of places to eat with fresh, tasty food. It wasn't perfect - it rained heavily most afternoons, could be very hot some mornings and was often very busy with tourists - but it came close. We ended up extending our stay three times.

Running wasn't always easy in Hoi-an but early rises and a little planning ensured I got out to run most days. One of the best parts about running on holiday is that you get off the beaten track and see how daily life plays out far away from the busy streets and tourist bubble. I became familiar with outlying clusters of settlements where local farmers worked and raised their families. The kids would all wave, call out or run alongside me, but the parents and grandparents usually remained impassive under their traditional conical hats. They were working too hard to look up, toiling knee-deep in paddy-fields with only oxen to make their lives easier. The oldest generation were particularly small in stature but looked as tough as weathered bamboo, hardened by years working in all elements, dealing with whatever life threw at them. Their hard labour and basic homes were a stark contrast with the luxury afforded to me: running around for the fun of it. I have no doubt that most of them are still there, working and living as they have done for decades. The simplicity of their daily lives was humbling but I was grateful to be free to live the way I wanted.

Recovery: Your body is a puzzle for you to figure out

"To the wise life is a problem; to the fool, a solution."
(Marcus Aurelius)

How could my hamstring still be a problem? I had

run a marathon on it; why had it not healed? There were lots of questions bouncing around my head as I walked back to the hostel after being forced to cut short a morning run. Over two months had passed since I'd injured my hamstring and I had run a marathon in the meantime. I had done some quality runs already in Hoi-An, including two speed sessions, and had thought that I was getting stronger. Unfortunately, that assumption had proved to be mistaken. It was demoralising to have to walk back to the hotel, knowing that the injury was still holding me back. I had researched and tried every technique I could find to improve it. *I didn't deserve to be injured again.* The self-pity of a limping runner is hard to match. It was a blow to me at the time, but it was the starting point in changing my whole attitude to injury.

Instead of trying to find the cause of the injury, I had been trying to find a solution. Stretching and massaging the hamstring hadn't worked in the long term, so something else must be affecting it. I started asking myself why. *Why was it happening? When was it happening? What exactly was happening?* I had been looking at a few pieces of the puzzle without considering how they all fitted together.

Flicking through some photos on my camera, I noticed that my stance was similar in many of them: standing with my hands resting on the back of my hips, over-arching my lower back to compensate for my lazily-rounded shoulders. Whenever I sat for a long time and felt my shoulders and posture rounding, I would arch my lower back to compensate; one part of me was trying to balance out another. During long scooter rides that summer, my hamstring would ache and throb. Although the problems were in my leg, it all seemed to stem from my lower back. *That was it!* The more I read up about it, the more convinced I became that my incorrect posture was causing my injuries.

I thought about how my daily habits had changed in the last few years. My workplace had moved from a classroom to an office over the previous two years. I used to stand for most of the day but now I was sitting. At the same time, I had increased the physical demands I made on myself by running harder sessions for longer. The change had been so gradual that I had grown accustomed to it without realising how much of an adjustment it was for my body. I remembered how I would arch my back several times a day, feeling that I was compensating for the inevitable slouching of my back when typing or writing in my office chair. All I was doing, however, was moving from a rounded to an over-extended lower back posture. I had reacted to my pain and discomfort without examining the cause.

Once I had identified the problem, I started to address it. The most obvious change I made was to become more conscious of my posture throughout the day: tucking in my navel, walking taller and supporting my back by holding some tension around the middle of my body. My core training now focused on strengthening my lower back rather than letting my hamstrings do all the work while running. It wasn't a quick fix, but it targeted the cause rather than the effect. It was a little change that had major benefits.

CHAPTER 17: COMPETITION TIME

Performance: Competition should bring out the best in us

"Associate with those who will make a better man of you. Welcome those whom you yourself can improve."
(Seneca, Letters from a Stoic, 7.8)

<u>Training Diary: Training Review</u>
Nine weeks to Dublin marathon

Back in Ireland and back to the start. Got back home three weeks ago and ran my first 'long' run over 10 miles since the marathon. It's staggering to think that was almost three months ago. I felt heavy and sluggish at the start, but my endurance has really come on since. I ran 18 miles two weeks ago and 19 miles last week. The paces were slow, but I was surprised I had it in my legs. All the bits of training in Thailand seem to have added up. I've signed up for the Charleville half-marathon in three weeks to see where I really am. That will leave me six weeks to pick things up again for Dublin. I won't taper for Charleville but will give it everything I have on the day.

When I was booking the half-marathon, I was surprised at the range of pace groups for the race. In addition to the usual paces like 2:00 and 1:30, they also had a pacer at 1:20. When I saw that group, it was as if someone had laid out a challenge to take on my personal best of 1:23. On paper there was only a three-minute difference, but in practice I would have to run about eighteen seconds per mile faster (eleven seconds per kilometre). I would never have contemplated attempting that time on my own, but if there was going to be a sizeable group running at that pace, I could try to stay with them for a while. The risk was that I would overstretch myself and be pinged back to the next pacing group of 1:25. The other option was to run more conservatively and come in just under my PB. In the end, the lure of the challenge outweighed the risks. I would try to run as many 6:04 minute miles (3:46 per kilometre) as I could and see where I ended up. Races are there to be run and that's what I planned to do.

Race Report: Charleville Half-Marathon
Six weeks to Dublin marathon

After three miles, a 1:20 target didn't seem like the right plan. There was a group of around fifteen runners in front of me who all seemed more comfortable with the pace than I was. Clinging on at the back, I had only one runner next to me. I'm careful about judging anyone, especially a runner, on appearances but I knew this guy was working far too hard to keep up the pace. If I started to match his stride, I knew I would be cast adrift from the main group, but my legs felt too heavy to bridge the gap. I was running fast enough to be outside of my comfort zone but not fast enough to catch up with the group.

One mile on and the other runner at the back had dropped out. I was now on my own, trailing a few metres behind the main group. I asked myself if I was now that guy, going too fast and working too hard. A negative mind-set was beginning to creep in. *Was I risking my race just to stay with the group? Would I not be better off running at my own pace?* It was like a heavy cloak that was only slowing me down. I needed to get back to the grind and simply concentrate on running the distance. I gave myself short, snappy instructions: *shut up, breathe deep, look at the pacer, keep running.* It didn't become physically easier, but my mind quietened and I kept going.

When we passed the 10-km mark, I glanced at the digital clock at the side of the road. It read 37:35. I blinked a few times as I took in the time. It was faster than I had ever run ten kilometres. The last time I had run that distance was when I'd battled the beach in Clontarf. That was the lift I needed at the right time. I decided that I would really give it a go and hang on to the group for as long as possible. So, that's what I did: I hung on. The further I could keep that up, the less distance I'd have to cover when I would run out of steam.

All my thoughts were focused on getting closer to the back of the pacer's group. It simplified everything for me. *Stay within a few strides. Don't let them slip away.* As we approached a slightly downhill section, I nudged forward and wedged myself into the back of the group. Now, there were runners directly in front and to the sides. It was a calm morning so there was no breeze from which to shelter, but it felt like I was sharing the effort with the group. I looked ahead at the lone runner who had been in front of us since the very start. He had stayed ahead of us for so long, but I knew the power of the group was going to swallow him up. It was like a pack of wolves chasing down a single rabbit. If I could stay in the pack, I could harness that power.

I could now see the pacer clearly. He had the

appearance of what I had always imagined a distance runner to be: tall, with a lean build and rangy stride. Although I estimated his age to be in the mid-twenties, he looked like a classic 1980s runner with a curly mullet of hair tied back with a headband, retro athletic vest and shorts. As I got closer, I could hear him give advice and encouragement. He had a little bottle of water in each hand to pass on to the group as they needed them. His words were short and to the point as he called out distances, the gradient ahead and our finishing time, based on our current pace. "Bit slow on last mile lads, but we have a downhill coming up" or "that one was bang on six minutes, lads". Most of us would not have managed that pace on our own. This guy wasn't simply running in front of the group, he was leading it.

Running Tip: Run in blocks

I usually break up a half-marathon into five blocks. The first three blocks are 5 km each that I call *'sow, flow, go.'* The initial pace should be run slightly behind my target pace to get me warmed up but sow the seeds for the later blocks. The second 5 km is about getting a flow to my stride and handling the pace without feeling that I'm working too hard. I'm usually behind my target time at this point but the same effort should be returning faster splits. The *'go'* phase naturally steps up the pace as I edge towards a negative split – running the second half of the race faster. The fourth section, *'hold'*, is the most challenging section for me as I try to maintain the pace from the *'go'* phase and not think about the remaining six kilometres. I remind myself to just hold the pace for this short three-kilometre block. Once I have covered that phase, it's 3.1 km to *'race'* to the end and empty my legs of whatever is left. The *'race'* section is tough on the body, but my mind is stronger knowing the end is within reach.

I had completed the three 5-km sections and felt ready for the next block of distance. The pacer called out that it was going to be a fast one to balance out the splits. It was a downhill section with an easy gradient, but the pace was intense at this point. The physical demands focused my mind as I tried to stay with the momentum of the group, staring blankly at the shoulder of the runner in front of me. As we neared the end of this block and joined the main road leading us back from Limerick to Cork, some of the runners in front faded to the side and I drifted into the space in front of me. I was now beside the pacer. *How did I end up here?* I had been spluttering at the back for so long, yet now I was matching the pacer's stride as we powered along a stretch of main road. I felt lighter and stronger than at any other point in the race. A steep humpback bridge loomed ahead; another challenge on a day of many. I focused on nothing else but that bump on the road and once we were over it, I knew that we were in the last block of the race. All that was left was to empty the tank, and whatever that got me would be a bonus.

Looking at the pacer to my left, I thought it would be great to finish the race with him. Instead, I surprised myself by saying, "I think I've got a little bit left in me". *Jesus, what did I say that for?* He replied in his broad Limerick accent, "G'wan, biy, go for it!". *Feck, I can't back down now.* Nudging my way just ahead of the group, my inner critic, Cowboy Coach, was back and chuckling to himself, *you're gonna' make a damn fool of yourself, boy!* The prospect of dropping back and embarrassing myself was like a whip cracking just behind me. Nearing the end, another runner from the group joined me for a sprint-finish to the line. We had pushed so hard that I didn't know my time, although I knew it was good. I also knew that I was on the verge of vomiting; thankfully I managed to refrain, and my bent-over crab walk sufficed instead.

Later, when I spotted the pacer, I shook his hand and thanked him for leading the group. He had impressed me so much by the way he had brought people with him. His words and actions carried intent but also consideration for those around him. Recognising me, he said, "Great running, biy. How'd you do?" I replied, "I think I got 1:18!" He slapped me on the shoulder. "Great stuff, biy. You looked strong at the end." My time was confirmed later as a few seconds under 1:19; more importantly, it was the catalyst for a change in my self-confidence as a runner.

Challenges: Consider what it takes to commit

"Do you wish to win at Olympia? So do I, by the gods, for it is a fine thing. But consider the first steps to it, and the consequences, and so lay your hand to the work. You must submit to discipline, eat to order, touch no sweets, train under compulsion, at a fixed hour, in heat and cold, drink no cold water, nor wine, except by order; you must hand yourself over completely to your trainer as you would to a physician, and then when the contest comes you must risk getting hacked, and sometimes dislocate your hand, twist your ankle, swallow plenty of sand, sometimes get a flogging, and with all this suffer defeat. When you have considered all this well, then enter on the athlete's course, if you still wish it." (Epictetus, Enchiridion, 29)

What is a real runner? Surely, it's anyone who runs

regularly is one. I had already completed a marathon; wouldn't that automatically earn me the title of a real runner? But it wasn't until that half-marathon that I felt like one. It had nothing to do with the time or position – the race had attracted a strong field, so I was nowhere near the top. I knew something had changed but I still couldn't quite identify it. I thought back to the week before the Cork marathon. Angie and I had started out on the Saturday night going for food and ended up staying out for late drinks with another couple we had just met. It wasn't the worst thing in the world – nor the best – but I had taken pride in the fact that I was having my night out despite planning to run a marathon a few days later. I could have my pints along with a strong measure of bravado and still do the miles. I ran but I hadn't committed to being a runner.

It was only that September, after more than a full year of fairly consistent training, that I could say I was committing to running. It wasn't about extra miles or sessions. In fact, over the summer I had run less but, counterintuitively, I felt more like a runner. What was different was my mindset. Even though I was clocking fewer miles, I was doing the best I could to be a better runner. Sticking with Muay Thai training while taking punishment from Noi, running in the humidity of an Asian summer, drinking less and figuring out my injury, all reinforced the ingredients of endurance that I had learned as a teenager: knowledge, self-discipline, courage and consistency. In Charleville, I was able to reap the benefit of all that work by pushing myself and then holding my limits for every one of the 21,098 metres. My sense of satisfaction wasn't about the race times but rather my personal progress. I had set, and then committed, to my own expectations; I was beginning to live up to my potential.

Mindset: Don't compare yourself to others, be inspired by them

> *"Happy also is he who can so revere a man as to calm and regulate himself by calling him to mind! One who can so revere another, will soon be himself worthy of reverence." (Seneca, Letters from a Stoic, 11.9)*

      I used to compare myself to my own stereotypical image of a runner: club vest, short shorts, wiry, lean, possibly sporting a mullet. It was a silly comparison, as competitive runners come in all shapes and sizes. Now I was being inspired and encouraged by the example of other runners, instead of comparing myself to them. The way that pacer ran was more influential than the time he ran. He led, supported, inspired; he put time and effort into bringing others further and faster than they'd ever gone before.
      Another runner whom I had admired was a red-haired work colleague, 'Fox'. He only took up running in his late twenties but rarely did anything in moderation so after six months of training twice a day, clocking triple my weekly mileage, he ran 2:52 for his first, and only, marathon. At the time, I couldn't better that pace for half-marathons and thought I could never reach his level. I had elevated him to a different category that was off-limits for me. When I smashed my PB, I broke the glass walls I had built around myself and I wasn't going to box myself in any longer. Those guys summed up what a runner should be: someone who gives of themselves or gives their all. I wasn't looking up to them anymore but rather looking to see how I could learn from them.

Attitude: Face whatever you fear

"No prize-fighter can go with high spirits into the strife if he has never been beaten black and blue." (Seneca, Letters from a Stoic, 13.2)

What do runners fear most? In most cases, I would venture the guess that it's injury; having to stop doing what you love to do. Injury had seemed an ever-present prospect for the previous six months and had affected my approach to running. I was conservative, staying away from hills and running mostly on flat terrain. But Dublin wasn't going to be a flat marathon; I needed to taste some of what I was going to face.

With four weeks to the marathon, I had my last long run before tapering. It was to be a 20-miler (32 km) that would build after a few miles to 6:30 mile (4:03 km) pace. Instead of running my usual route by Blackrock castle, I followed a route with rolling hills like those in Dublin. I wanted to get my legs familiar with the extra stress of elevation when fatigued. I felt it was more important to replicate the course conditions than to run steady splits. Ideally, I would expend the same amount of effort on both the incline and decline, in the hope that the pace would balance out. 'Hold the hills' was my cue to keep my efforts consistent both uphill and downhill.

I even began the run at the same time as I would start in Dublin, 9:00 a.m. I started out slowly, my pace varying throughout according to elevation. Although the average pace was below target for the session – over 6:40 per mile – my last two miles were the fastest at 6:21 per mile. I had faced my weakness and finished strongly.

Hitting my target paces on flat ground would have looked neater on paper but doubts about taking on the hills would have remained. Having those twenty miles in my legs gave me a lingering feeling of satisfaction over the tapering period.

Running Tip: Hold the Hills

When I run uphill, my stride becomes much shorter, my feet land under my body and my hips and arms work harder to drive me forward. I look to the crest of the hill to keep running tall. It's a reminder of good running form. Even though it's tough, it makes me run stronger and better.

Routine: Dig deep to find space for bigger blocks

"It is not that we have a short time to live, but that we waste a lot of it. Life is long enough, and a sufficiently generous amount has been given to us for the highest of achievements if it were all well invested." (Seneca, On the Shortness of Life, 1.4)

Although I was now happier with my effort in running, I was struggling to get that kind of consistency in other areas. I was wedging core-work, cross-training, reading and writing into random parts of the day or pushing them over to the next one. More importantly, I wasn't making enough time for Angie. Over the summer, I had lost the habit of training before work. I needed to find time in my day again. Listening to a podcast called '5 a.m. miracle' was just the motivation I needed to start setting my alarm a little earlier each day, going from 6:50am to 6:25am; those extra few minutes made a significant difference. It meant getting my run done earlier in the day and was much more likely to do some cross-training or core-work that evening as well. Getting up early made me more determined to make better use of my time. There was no point in rising early in the morning if I wasted my time in the evening. The earlier mornings meant a bedtime of around 10:30 p.m. but demanding more returned more.

Training Diary: Tearing up the Tempo
Five weeks to Dublin marathon

Tempo Session Review: Ran well under the target of 6:40 per mile (4:08 per km) this evening. Was surprised at how easy the effort felt. Had to ease off at the end. Things seem to be coming together.

Training Diary: Long Run with some Hills
Two weeks to Dublin marathon
Target Run: Long run of thirteen miles at 6:34 per mile pace (4:05 per km)

Review: Ran 13.1 miles at 6:37 per mile (4:07 per km) pace which made it just under 1:27 for a half-marathon. More than the time and paces, I'm happy with my effort. I felt strong even though I went out of my way to incorporate some rolling hills and felt comfortable running them. Dublin isn't as flat as the routes I've been training on, so it was a great boost to my confidence to know that I can take on the hills.

CHAPTER 18: COUNTDOWN TO DCM

Routine: A good routine only needs small changes

"Be careful, however, lest this reading of many authors and books of every sort may tend to make you discursive and unsteady. You must linger among a limited number of master thinkers, and digest their works, if you would derive ideas which shall win firm hold in your mind. Everywhere means nowhere." (Seneca, Letters from a Stoic, 2.2)

On my long runs leading up to the taper, I tried to follow a similar routine with little adjustments and improvements each time such as when and what to eat, when to go for a warm-up jog and when to stretch. My breakfast for long runs or races was almost always the same: porridge oats with water and some milk simmered on the stove for ten minutes before adding a handful of berries and roasted nuts. It was simple and filling and as they might say in Cork, "it's hard to bate the porridge, biy". Having a consistent routine freed my mind from making too many decisions and let me focus more on getting ready to run. Likewise, the tapering period isn't the time to make any major changes to a routine and I was about to find out why.

Tapering for a marathon leads to an excess of time, thoughts and energy. It's a heady mix that can be a struggle to channel in the right way. With less miles to cover, I started to read different resources on stretching and mobility and introduced an evening stretching routine. It seemed to go well until I stepped out into a lunge and felt a twinge in a groin muscle. My body hadn't been warm enough to be stretched into an unfamiliar position. Instead of reading from different sources and adding new exercises, I should have stuck to what was familiar so close to the race.

I had to skip the long run that weekend. Trying to do too much had made it difficult to do anything. Getting up in cold morning darkness is much more challenging when you're not sure what you should be doing. *Should I rest or run?* The tapering period can feel strange enough as it is: doing less to do more. Doing nothing at all was even tougher, but it wasn't worth the risk of aggravating the injury any further.

Recovery: Keep your head and do your best

"Keep your head. Our busy minds are forever jumping to conclusions, manufacturing and interpreting signs that aren't there. Assume, instead, that everything that happens to you does so for some good. That if you decided to be lucky, you are lucky." (Epictetus, Enchiridion)

A few days of easy running and I felt stronger again. I tried to remain positive. *Maybe I needed a week's rest. It was only a slight injury. At least I can run.* I ignored the programme and just ran what I could for that week. I've included some entries from my training diary from that week.

<u>Training Diary: Getting Speed and Confidence Back</u>
One week to Dublin

Review: Training has been broken up since injury last week and I had to skip the long run and speed session, so did some very light jogging instead. The last three mornings, I ran around five kilometres under marathon pace (6:29 per mile/ 4:02 per km). I'm feeling more confident about being ready to run.

<u>Training Diary: Race Plan</u>
One day to go

I'm aware of the marathon route but don't know it as well as I'd like. I know there's a tough hill that comes at a challenging stage of the race, around mile 22. Apart from that, I'm just going to run it as best I can. My goal, set back in June, was to run a sub-3-hour marathon, but I feel that's not my main target now. My 'B' target is to run a sub-2:55 with a dream target of chasing the Fox at 2:52. I feel strong and am looking forward to the next time I write here.

CHAPTER 19: MARATHON REVIEW

Challenges: Anything worthwhile takes some pain to achieve

"Pleasure is not the reward or the cause of virtue but comes in addition to it." (Seneca, On a Happy Life, Book 9)

Post-marathon aches and pains meant I was walking backwards down stairs for days. The stiffness was sore yet satisfying and stayed with me as we travelled up to County Antrim for a few days. I was probably one of the few people ever to come down from the Giant's Causeway by walking backwards. Slow walks, hot pies and cold beers were all enlisted to aid my recovery. Despite the soreness in my legs, I felt high in energy for most of the week and woke at dawn each day.

<u>*Journal: Post-Marathon High*</u>
Three days after the marathon

Today is our last day in the penthouse apartment in Belfast. I haven't slept much the last few nights; still high from Monday. I got up around 5:00 a.m. to admire the peaceful cityscape of Belfast as the darkness of the night changed to the blue light of dawn and then the bright light of early morn. For hours now, I've been drinking strong coffee, writing and staring out through the floor-to-ceiling windows of the apartment. My third cup warms and invigorates me. I cast my mind back to Dublin and the glow of satisfaction is still there.

Race Report: Dublin Marathon

Shit, why can't I get my legs going? I wasn't wearing a GPS watch, but I knew that my pace was sluggish. Just a few miles in, my dream target of running under 2:52 seemed to be slipping away. I wasn't running anywhere near the 6:34 per mile (4:05 per km) required. I was willing my legs to go faster but it felt like I was working hard just to stay close to my main target pace of 6:40 per mile (4:08 per km). After resting for the two days leading up to the race and the three-hour drive the day before, my legs felt dull and heavy. It was disappointing to realise my times were lagging but my goal-paces were meant to be pushing me on, not weighing me down. I needed to let them go and get back to doing my best.

By the time I had covered six miles, I was beginning to feel a little looser but was still well off my dream target pace. When I looked back at the race website after the race, I could see that I was chip-timed coming through the 10-km mark in 41:33 at 6:42 per mile, just over 2:55 pace. For the next ten kilometres, I just focused on my form and breathing. My stride began to flow a little more smoothly, but it was still hard to lift the pace. I passed through halfway in 1:27:28 which was exactly my 'B' target pace. A sub-3-hour time looked like a safe bet if my legs didn't seize up. My dream target seemed like a balloon floating ever further out of reach, but a sub-2:55 time looked achievable. All I had to do was hold steady, but instead I tried to reach higher and push harder.

Second half, new race. Targets, injuries and heavy legs didn't matter any longer. Competing against a name, a face, a friend can inspire greater motivation than running against a time. An obstinate mix of determination and pettiness drove me on to chase the Fox and his PB.

Inclines and doubts duly popped up but repeating the words, *this will pass*, reminded me that pain and hills never last. Running through the villages of Crumlin and Dolphin's Barn, with supporters out in force, lifted me when I needed it most. I knew I was running faster but was too tired to figure out my splits. A GPS watch would have told me that I was edging towards my dream target pace, reaching the 30-km mark in 2:04:02 at 6:37 per mile pace.

Running faster felt great but I had to balance that burst of enthusiasm with the prospect of Roebuck Road, Dublin's version of 'Heartbreak Hill', still waiting to test me at mile 22. Even though I was trying to pick up the pace, the prospect of running that hill ensured I didn't dig too deep too early. When the hill did appear, it wasn't anywhere near as bad as I'd thought it would be. If anything, it had acted as a form of pacemaker to curb my enthusiasm until the very last section.

Once I'd got over that hill, I knew that I just had half an hour of running to see how much I had in reserve. When I hit Foster's Avenue, I took advantage of the downhill gradient to push as hard as I could. It was worth the sore quad muscles it earned me for the rest of the week. My exuberance was soon brought back to the grind of the miles as we dipped into a quieter section of the course by University College Dublin, where there were only beeping cars in support. I was running on my own and like a heavy shower of rain, discomfort and pain were soaking every part of me.

The course rose up and led into a more residential area, Nutley Lane. Pain continued to rain down, but supporters gave shelter from the storm. Smiles and cardboard posters with funny lines helped clear the dark skies; 'Run faster, I just farted,' was one of the best. Just a mile was left as I ran down Merrion Road. Supporters leaned over fences on either side to clap us onwards. It was like going through a tunnel of noise and emotion with deliverance waiting on the other side. The crowds elevated me above the pain and I began to sprint. Beaming a broad smile, I held my arms out to the side. A photographer captured me in full flight.

It felt as if I could have run forever, until I hit the soft foam padding leading up to the finish line. It suddenly felt as if my legs no longer belonged to me, but I borrowed them back for one last push to the end and then it was over: 2:54:03. The second half was nearly a minute faster than the first.

I wobbled my way through the finishing area with my hands clasped on the top of my head; jelly-legs with glazed eyes. The memories still tingle: trees and red-brick Georgian houses, laughter as I genuflected to receive my medal, easy chats and mutual congratulations with other runners, and Angie and my sister waiting with smiles and hugs at the end.

Courage: Are you ready?

"Remember that the contest is now, and that the

Olympic games are now, and that it is no longer possible to delay the match, and that progress is lost and saved as a result of one defeat and even one moment of giving in."
(Epictetus, Enchiridion, 51.2)

Satisfaction and caffeine fuelled me for days after the marathon. I wanted more but I tried not to think too far ahead. Whatever I did next, I needed to be ready to commit to it. It made sense to take it easy over the winter and build up a base of miles before sharpening up again on the brighter mornings of Spring. But runners often don't take the sensible option. Instead, I signed up for another marathon. Nine months after my first one, I would be back for my third in Barcelona on St. Patrick's weekend. It's taken a long time to run and write this story, but I haven't taken a backward step ever since.

Now it's time to run your story.

Epilogue

As I write this, it's three years later and I'm still running. The year of training covered in this book has stood to me ever since. The lessons I've learned have kept me going when I've struggled and made me go the long way around when I've tried to cut corners. The mental and physical training paid off when I ran 2:47 for the Barcelona marathon, just nine months after my first one in Cork.

Even though my times have improved, running has become more social. I finally caught up with Dinger and trained for much of my last marathon with him as we pushed each other right to the finish line and to personal bests. I still see the Monk at local races and my nickname proved to be uncannily accurate when he discussed the benefits of flagellation after one event. Joining a running club has been my second-best decision since taking up running. It has brought more enjoyment and healthy competition than I could have imagined. Cowboy Coach is long gone these days and has been replaced by our Olympian coach.

The best decision I've made since focusing on running was marrying Angie. She has had to find her own sense of endurance during my training for running, and then writing about running, while supporting me through five marathons. She also ran one of her own before her running career had to be cut short due to a stress fracture. She now cycles instead.

Author's Note

As a runner with a full-time job, much of the book has been written or edited while drinking coffee in our kitchen in the dark hours of early morning. Many critical eyes have looked over the words on these pages but despite my efforts and those of others, there may still be some typos or skewed formatting. I hope they don't distract from a book which is intended to help you become a better athlete.

As a self-publisher, I don't have the support of a big publishing house to promote this book. If you could write a review, it would be a huge boost to help the book stand out amid the Amazon pile and let other runners see what it has to offer. I know it can be awkward to remember and take the time when reading on Kindle, but even a one-line comment would make a big difference.

If you would like to send me a message or keep up to date with any future book releases (nothing planned yet!), my Facebook profile can be found at 'Stoic Runner' or you can email me at 'runlikeastoic@gmail.com'.

APPENDIX: OVERCOMING CHALLENGES

Lessons from Dublin Marathon

When I read books by endurance athletes like Dean Karnazes and Gerry Duffy, I'm fascinated to learn how they think and train. Completing ten Ironman triathlons in ten days and running fifty marathons in fifty North American states in fifty days are just two examples of the many feats they have accomplished. While I couldn't fathom putting my body through that kind of suffering, I could see how easy is to be swept from one feat to the next in a never-ending cycle of challenges. But like closing a book, it can be too easy just to move on and start afresh while missing all the lessons learned along the way. The warm glow of finishing a marathon fades but we should be left with enough embers to keep us going; we might need them in darker times ahead.

Before thoughts drifted to the next marathon challenge, I sat down to write what I had learned from this training cycle about overcoming challenges. It's heavy on Stoicism so that's why I have put it in the appendix at the back of this book. You might not want, or be ready, to read it now but you know where it is if you do.

How can we overcome challenges and learn from them?

Based on marathon training and reading Stoicism, I have tried to break down the steps that I feel are most useful in overcoming challenges. However, knowing the steps doesn't mean I always take them. It's still sometimes hard for me to put the theory into practice. Strong emotions, such as disappointment or anger, have blocked me from seeing clearly, accepting and moving on. Like cues for running, these are reminders of the steps I need to take to overcome challenges.

Stoic Resilience: Anticipate

"The unprepared are panic-stricken even at the most trifling things. We must see to it that nothing shall come upon us unforeseen. And since things are all the more serious when they are unfamiliar, continual reflection will give you the power, no matter what the evil may be, not to play the unschooled boy." (Seneca, Letters from a Stoic, 107.4)

Train in, and visualise, different conditions to prepare for whatever race day throws at you. Anticipate that things might not go to plan.

Anticipate: Expect the best, prepare for the worst

"But the man who is not puffed up in good times does not collapse either when they change. His fortitude is already tested, and he maintains a mind unconquered in the face of either condition." (Seneca, On the Shortness of Life, 5)

Action Steps
- Expect the best but prepare for the worst. Don't dwell too long on either.

Consider all outcomes and train all conditions to strengthen mind and body. You cannot control your fate, but you can ready yourself for whatever it throws at you. Reminding myself of the prospect of injury steers me away from injury; it makes me choose 'prehabilitation' instead of rehabilitation.

Anticipate: Everything good takes time and effort

"Nothing great is produced suddenly, since not even the grape or the fig is. If you say to me now that you want a fig, I will answer to you that it requires time: let it flower first, then put forth fruit, and then ripen."
(Epictetus, Discourses, 1.15)

Action Steps
- Make the time and take the effort to learn from the process.
- Be strong enough to be patient. Take it easy and get it right.

Sometimes getting better means going slower. For a runner's ego, that can be very challenging. If we take short-cuts, or skip steps, they will eventually send us back to the start. If we take our time, not only will we improve but we will get better at improving.

Anticipate: Find a coach, mentor or role model

> *"Choose a master whose life, conversation, and soul-expressing face have satisfied you; picture him always to yourself as your protector or your pattern. For we must indeed have someone according to whom we may regulate our characters."* (Seneca)

<u>Action Steps</u>
- Find a coach, mentor or role model to stay training consistently well.

Anticipate that you will lose your way at some point. A coach or mentor to give you objective support can be invaluable but if we don't, Seneca encourages us to choose role models to guide our thoughts and actions. Whenever you feel your attitudes or actions are weak, distracted or over-emotional, ask yourself how your role models would think or behave. I still believe we need to make our own mistakes sometimes but having someone by your side can get you where you want to go with fewer detours.

Stoic Resilience: Accept

> *"If it's endurable, endure it."* (Marcus Aurelius, Mediations, 10.3)

We cannot give our best if we do not accept our current circumstances. The hardship of bad weather and tough conditions won't hurt us but enduring them will make us stronger. Being better in the future must start with accepting whatever we face in the present.

Accept your present to better your future

"The untrained brood about the constituent elements of their lives. They waste precious time in regret or wishing their particulars were different ("If only I lived in a better house or town, had a different spouse, a more glamorous job, more time to myself...") The morally trained, rather than resenting or dodging their current life situations and duties, give thanks for them and fully immerse themselves in their duties to their family, friends, neighbors, and job. When we succumb to whining, we diminish our possibilities." (Epictetus, The Art of Living)

Action Steps
- Be emotional for as long as it helps to heal but accept that you eventually need to let it go to move on.

When life goes against us we might need to cry or curse, or both. However, it is only when we can accept our fitness, our ability, our fate that we can begin to move on.

Accept: Appreciate that all things come to an end

"Imagine that you're entering a festival each day and preparing yourself to endure the rough and tumble, but also to appreciate the spectacle while all the time accepting that certain, it must all come to an end, and that you must take nothing for granted." (Epictetus)

Action Steps
- Accept that everything must come to an end. Take nothing for granted.

Accept that you might not always be able to run. If you do that, you will never fail to appreciate it when you can.

Accept that you might need help

> *"Don't be ashamed of needing help. You have a duty to fulfil just like a soldier on the wall of battle. So what if you are injured and can't climb up without another soldier's help?" (Marcus Aurelius)*

Action Steps
- If you need help, be strong enough to ask for it.

It takes wisdom and bravery to accept that you have exhausted your own resources and that you need support. You might just need a leg-up from a club-mate, coach or counsellor to climb whatever wall you are facing. The worst we can do is not to ask.

Stoic Resilience: Adapt

> *"A flourishing life depends on our responding, as best we can, to those things uniquely incumbent upon us." (Epictetus)*

Just because we accept our circumstances like a Stoic, it doesn't mean that we should be passive. Instead, we must adapt and make ourselves stronger through whatever we face. As runners, it's about reacting in the best way we can to the conditions we experience.

Adapt: Become stronger through adversity

> *"Disaster is virtue's opportunity." (Seneca)*

Action Steps

- Treat challenges as opportunities.

Readiness to accept and adapt can turn stumbling blocks into building blocks. It may take time, but you can grow stronger from your failures than your successes if you see every disaster as an opportunity. Being injured is a chance to come back stronger mentally and physically.

Adapt: Test and adapt to keep growing

"The trials we endure can and should introduce us to our strengths. Prudent people look beyond the incident itself and seek to form habits of putting it to good use." (Epictetus)

Action Steps
- Test, learn, change, try again.

When you adapt through a process of trial and error, you make yourself stronger for another day. Without challenge and change, you cannot grow and develop. Every time we race or even train is a chance to improve our habits, preparation and practice.

Adapt: Dig deep from within

"Don't just react in a haphazard fashion; remember to turn inward and ask what resources you have for dealing with it. Dig deeply. You possess strengths you might not realise you have. Find the right one. Use it." (Epictetus)

Action Steps

- Ask yourself: what do I have to overcome this? Dig deep and come back with answers.

Stoicism encourages you to square up to all challenges by starting with yourself. It's easier to look online for quick answers that are surface-deep but it's much harder to delve down and ask to what extent you are at fault. Injuries are almost always our fault and it was only by asking myself harder questions that I got better answers.

Stoic Resilience: Act

> *"You must learn first and then strengthen your learning by action." (Seneca)*

Learn first, then put it into practice: learn, do, learn better, do better, repeat.

Act: Be mindful of your thoughts and behaviour

> *"You cannot correct that which you do not know you're doing incorrectly. You must catch your mistake before you can fix it." (Seneca, Letters from a Stoic, 28.10)*

<u>Action Steps</u>
- Review your day. Track your training.

Reviewing the positives and negatives from each day helps to redirect me for the next. Being more mindful of my mistakes means I'm less likely to repeat them in the future. Keeping a training journal highlights what I'm doing well and where I need to keep improving.

Act with integrity

"Indeed, nobody else can thwart the inner purposes of the mind. For it no fire can touch, nor steel, nor tyrant, nor public censure, nor anything whatsoever: a sphere once formed continues round and true." (Marcus Aurelius, Meditations, 8.41)

Action Steps
- Keep your shape no matter what happens or how badly you want something.

We should always endeavour to act, speak and think in a way that is reflective of who we are or who we strive to be. Cheating is one way we can lose before we even begin.

Act: Rest to refresh

"The liveliness of our minds will be destroyed by unceasing labour, but they will recover their strength after a short period of rest and relief: for continuous toil produces a sort of numbness and sluggishness." (Seneca, Of Peace of Mind)

Action Steps
- Train hard and then recover to come back stronger.
- Vary your training to refresh your body and mind.

Act: Learn to see events from a different viewpoint

"Men are disturbed not by things, but by the views which they take of them." (Epictetus)

Action Steps
- When you face misfortune, take a deep breath, accept how you feel before acknowledging yourself how much worse things could be.

It is up to us how we view the world we live in, but it is when we feel at our worst that we are often the most short-sighted. If I really struggle to initiate positive thoughts or actions, that's when I use negative visualisation to cut right through self-pity with a more severe version of whatever I face: being injured means I'm healthy enough to be only concerned about a running injury.

Act: Find a way to filter out negative thinking, worry and anxiety

> *"They lose the day in expectation of the night, and the night in fear of the dawn." (Seneca, On the Shortness of Life, 16.5)*

Action Steps
- Filter your thoughts. Ask yourself are they true, fair or helpful? Do whatever you can – talk, write, run – to filter out negative thoughts.

Negative thinking does not have the same benefits as negative visualisation: one closes our mind, the other opens it. Worry and anxiety are states of mind that can drain you of the very resources you need at the most demanding times. They will push doubt and dread into the cracks in your ego until they slow you to a stop. Like weeds, you need to try to prevent them from appearing or pluck them out before they take root. Get support if you feel you need it.

Act: Stay in the present

"Don't disturb yourself by thinking of the whole of your life. Don't let your thoughts embrace all the various troubles that you may expect, but on every occasion, ask yourself: what in this is past bearing? Next, remember that neither the past nor the future pains you, only the present, and this can be reduced to very little if only you will circumscribe it and chide your mind to hold out against so little." (Marcus Aurelius, Meditations, 8.36)

Action Steps
- Repeat throughout the day: What is the most important thing I can do right now?'

Once we know where we are going, the present is all that matters. Goals and targets are great to have, but it is only our actions in the present that will achieve them.

Act: Test your limits and weaknesses

"He is most powerful who has power over himself." (Seneca)

Action Steps
- Train your weaknesses. Get familiar with what you fear or lack.

The more we work on our weaknesses, the better we get at overcoming them.

Act: Enjoy what you do

A Stoic should have "a joy that is deep and issues from deep within, since he finds delight in his own resources, and desires no joys greater than his inner joys." (Seneca, Of a Happy Life)

Action Steps
- Do what you enjoy and enjoy what you do; otherwise you need to change direction.

All this philosophical talk gets a little heavy sometimes. We should never forget that we should enjoy what we do. I almost always feel happier when I come back from run. Results and benefits will not be sustainable if we don't derive inner joy from the process of getting them. It's not always going to be comfortable, but we are far more likely to achieve our potential if we enjoy what we do.

Stoic Resilience: Adjust

"But in life what do I do? What today I say is good, tomorrow I will swear is bad. And the reason is that, compared to what I know about logic, my knowledge and experience of life fall far behind." (Seneca, Discourses II, 3.4-5)

The knowledge you gain through experience should be forever testing your logic and beliefs. Every race should bring a little more clarity and focus to your training. This can mean changing perspective if your experiences provide you with a better point of view.

Adjust: Test the theory
"The living voice and the intimacy of a common life will help you more than the written word. You must

go to the scene of action." (Seneca, Letters from a Stoic, 6.5)

Action Steps
- Put into practice whatever you learn.

The true value of theory is to make it work for you. There is no one perfect plan to suit everyone. You are the only person who can test the theory to make it right for you.

Adjust: Be prepared to go back to basics

"But neither a bull nor a noble-spirited man comes to be what he is all at once; he must undertake hard winter training, and prepare himself, and not propel himself rashly into what is not appropriate to him."
(Epictetus)

Action Steps
- Go slow, get better and build from there. Take your time to get the basics right: how you run, sit, move, eat, sleep, drink, think.

How many of us run injury-free? How many of us are mindful of our form every time we run? When pain and twinges become the norm, it means we need to go back to basics.

Adjust: Remind yourself to be grateful

"All you need are these: certainty of judgement in the present moment; action for the common good in the present moment; and an attitude of gratitude in the

present moment for anything that comes your way."
(Marcus Aurelius, Meditations, 9.6)

Action Steps
- When you're disappointed by external events, remind yourself to be grateful that you had the chance to try.

The Stoics believed that gratitude reminds us to be thankful for what we have. If we fail the first time at something, we should be grateful for the opportunity to learn from it and try again. Another day will bring another challenge. Being disappointed by race times shouldn't be tolerated when we are healthy enough to run, compete and try again.

Adjust: Living well is a continual process

"Begin at once to live and count each separate day as a separate life." (Seneca, Letters from a Stoic, 101.10)

Action Steps
- Treat every day as a fresh start to do things right.

If today didn't go so well, tomorrow is another chance to try again.

Adjust: Grow through pain

"To bear this worthily is good fortune." (Marcus Aurelius, Meditations)

Action Steps

- Take away comfort to add strength: train tough to run easy.
- Remember that pain will pass but know the difference between hurt and pain.

Modern life typically strives for more luxury, comfort and convenience. We can become accustomed to obtaining things easily and grow unfamiliar with the hardship that is necessary to build endurance. The Stoics believed that we should deliberately experience discomfort to take away the fear of pain and train our ability to endure.

Training in all conditions not only accustoms us to the discomfort of cold, humidity and heat but also takes away the fear of it in the future. Much like getting into cold water, once you get over the initial shock you won't understand how you thought it was so bad at first. If you can stay with the pain until it passes, you will have developed both your physical ability to tolerate discomfort and your mental capacity to resist it. If we give up or always look for the easy way out, our minds will always look for that trapdoor for us to escape.

Growth requires pain at some point, but our bodies will warn us if we push it too hard and we must respect that. Hurt injures, pain strengthens. If you're ever unsure whether it's pain or hurt, ask yourself: Will this make me weaker or stronger?

Bibliography/ Reading List

The resources that I've used for this book are all from the ancient texts of Stoic philosophers. They are freely available online but some of the older translations can be a little cumbersome to read. If you only read one original Stoic text, my recommendation would be to start with *Letters from a Stoic* by Seneca. It's a book I return to read every few months and is more like a series of short essays on different themes than a series of letters. The best translation is by Robin Campbell, but older translations are available in the public domain and can be found on Wikipedia.

If I had to recommend a second Stoic book to read, my choice would be *Meditations* by Marcus Aurelius. It is a personal journal so doesn't read quite as well as Seneca's books, in my opinion, but is a thought-provoking insight into the mindset of the most powerful man in the world at that time. To give you an idea of his humility, the first part is a gratitude journal where he gives thanks to the people in his life who have made him who he is. Gregory Hayes has written the most readable translation for the Modern Library. Another excellent book to start with is The Shortness of Life by Seneca, which has a modern version published by Penguin Books.

Once you become more comfortable with the stark clarity of Stoicism, you could delve into the works of Epictetus. Two of his books, Enchiridion and Discourses, contain some staggering pieces of life advice. He lived a tough life and likewise some of his language can be hard to read but he is worth sticking with; Enchiridion means handbook and is meant as something to keep at hand and return to over time.

Acknowledgements

To the many people who have read over and given me honest feedback, I can't thank you enough especially John O' Regan, Christopher Lee and Rick Matz. I was very lucky to find such a skilled editor in Elaine Kennedy, and any mistakes are not of her making but my own tampering and editing up until the last minute before publishing.

To my family for all living their part in the story behind the book and playing their part in helping me to write about it after. Mum and Dad for just being such a positive influence in my life. Claire, the cover looks amazing and hopefully people will judge the book by it in this case. Grace, I kept it secret so long, I didn't give a chance to help as much as I know you could have (I'll know for next time!). Fiona, your critical feedback and insights were especially appreciated in improving my writing and I believe it's a better book because of you.

Most of all, I want to thank you Angie for not only enduring life with a runner but one who also tries to be a writer. Your love and support has shown me how to be a better man.